URBAN INEQUALITY AND HOUSING
POLICY IN TANZANIA

Urban Inequality and Housing Policy in Tanzania

THE PROBLEM OF SQUATTING

RICHARD E. STREN

Institute of International Studies
University of California, Berkeley

International Standard Book Number 0-87725-124-X
Library of Congress Card Number 75-620118

ACKNOWLEDGMENTS

This study originated in Tanzania in 1972-73 when, as the officer in charge of the Planning Unit of the Ministry of Lands, Housing and Urban Development, I was privileged to work under Mr. Bernard Sikilo, the Principal Secretary. His enthusiasm and intelligent guidance were extremely important in directing me toward an appreciation of the squatter problem that was in keeping with Tanzania's socialist policies. During my stay in Dar es Salaam, I learned a great deal from Dr. Robert Merrill, then the Housing Finance Advisor to the Ministry, about the economics of sites and services schemes, and the international experience with various kinds of low-cost housing programs. I am also in the debt of Mr. S.M. Nyamgunda, who tirelessly took me around the squatter areas in Dar es Salaam, discussing the problems of these areas with me and making it possible for me to talk with many Tanzanian "squatters" who had very definite ideas about what the government ought to do. To Manfred Bienefeld and Richard Sabot go special thanks for allowing me to use their NUMEIST survey data to examine the socio-economic characteristics of the Dar es Salaam population; Chapter IV of this study would not have been possible without their help.

After I left Dar es Salaam, a research grant from the Canada Council made it possible for me to reflect on the Tanzanian problem from a more comparative perspective. When, more recently, I decided to write up my material in its present form, Mr. Raymond Catchpole and Professor Gerald Helleiner were kind enough to offer helpful suggestions for the strengthening of various parts of the argument. At the end of the whole process, I have become very conscious of the degree to which my clumsy text has been improved by the adept editorial hand of Mr. Paul Gilchrist.

Finally, I would like to record here my gratitude to my wife, Gladys, who lived through a lot while this study was taking shape, and who is more than anyone entitled to the credit for any merit it may have.

R.E.S.

October 1975
Toronto, Canada

CONTENTS

LIST OF TABLES

INTRODUCTION

Two striking features of contemporary urbanization in
the Third World are the extraordinarily rapid rates of growth
of the large cities, and the increasingly large proportion of
the population living in poor housing or badly serviced areas.
The United Nations has projected an annual rate of urban growth
in the Third World of 4.1 percent between 1960 and 2000, with
a corresponding increase in the rural population of 1.8 percent.[1] This rate of urban growth would be higher than that
experienced by any developed region except North America between
1850 and 1920.[2] At this pace, Third World countries as a whole
will be 22 percent urbanized in 1980, as against 15 percent in
1960.[3] Latin America will be the most urbanized continent in
the Third World; Africa, the least. At present, however, the
African continent probably has the highest rate of urban growth
in the world.

In large part because of this rapid urban growth, more
and more people are crowding into poor and unsanitary housing.
Thus a recent study of slum and squatter conditions in large
cities showed that in Istanbul 45 percent of the population
lived in "slums and uncontrolled settlements." The corresponding figures for other major centers were: Lagos, 43 percent;
Caracas, 42 percent; Lima, 36 percent; Manila, 34 percent;
Kuala Lumpur, 30 percent; Bandung, 27 percent; and Seoul, 24
percent.[4] Another survey of the major cities in forty developing
countries showed that in 17 of these cities more than half of
the populations were living in "slums and uncontrolled settlements," while in only 12 were less than a third of the people
living in such areas.[5] In many large cities, the growth in

---

[1]The World Bank, Urbanization: Sector Working Paper (Washington, 1972), p. 12.

[2]Paul Bairoch, Urban Unemployment in Developing Countries
(Geneva: International Labour Organization, 1973), p. 19.

[3]The World Bank, Urbanization . . ., p. 12.

[4]Canadian International Development Agency, Cooperation Canada,
No. 16 (September/October 1974), p. 16.

[5]Hollis Chenery et al., Redistribution with Growth (London:
Oxford University Press, 1974), p. 151n.

"shantytown" populations is estimated at over 20 percent a year,[6] which would lead to their doubling in less than four years.

These growth features have been clearly documented, but there are substantial differences of opinion among scholars and policymakers concerning how best to deal with the problems created by rapid urban growth--in particular, the "problem" of squatting. Some of these differences can best be understood as resulting from different perspectives concerning what constitutes the main aspect of the squatting "problem." Following an examination of these different perspectives in Chapter I, we shall turn our attention to a case study of Dar es Salaam-- the capital of Tanzania. Tanzania is of particular interest because it is one of the few Third World countries that have explicitly attempted to implement policies designed to reduce both urban/rural inequalities and inequalities within the urban areas themselves. These policies may be beneficial in other respects (as we shall see), but they have failed to arrest the growth of squatting. An analysis of the reasons for the growth of squatting in Dar es Salaam, together with some survey data on the squatters themselves, suggests some of the factors underlying the gap between policy intentions and actual results.

In the concluding section of this study, we shall make some modest proposals for policies which may help to reduce the problem of squatting to manageable proportions.

---

[6]The World Bank, _Urbanization_ . . ., p. 17.

Chapter I

SQUATTING IN THE THIRD WORLD:
A DIVERSITY OF PROBLEMS - A CONVERGENCE OF SOLUTIONS

Squatting has been seen as a "problem" by both Western
and Third World planners. Despite a diversity of views concerning what constitutes the most important aspect of the problem,
a consensus is emerging which sees the solution to squatting in
overall strategies rather than piecemeal solutions. In the
following discussion this emerging consensus is presented by
analyzing squatting in terms of four main problem areas: political, social, economic, and physical.

A. Squatting as a Political Problem

A number of authorities have argued that urban slums
and squatter areas are likely to be an important source of
political instability. Charles Abrams, for example, has compared
Third World urban conditions with the "pre-revolutionary" situation in nineteenth-century Europe described by Marx:

There is no more fertile ground for revolutionary propaganda
than the beleaguered cities of the underdeveloped nations.
Misery, bitterness, and resentment in the teeming slums
and squatter colonies, low wages and long hours in the new
factories, competition for jobs, and child labor, all recall
the scene that made the Communist Manifesto an alluring
document in nineteenth-century Europe.
   In Western Europe, communism bowed to reform. Europe
weathered the shift to industrialization because there were
frontiers to absorb some of the surplus people; institutional roots were more settled; conservative churches counseled
prayer, not rebellion; and there was a strong shop-keeper-
handicraft economy willing to tolerate change but not
revolution.
   These buffers are missing in industrializing Asia,
Africa, and Latin America. Street sleeping, homelessness,
and over-crowding are incomparably worse than anything
Marx described in London's East End. . . .[1]

---

[1]Man's Struggle for Shelter in an Urbanizing World (Cambridge,
Mass.: M.I.T. Press, 1966), p. 287.

3

Abrams observes elsewhere that "Squatter areas breed many things in many parts of the world: sullenness, hatred of authority, and violation of law are only a few."[2]

Even more sweeping is this oft-quoted passage from Barbara Ward:

> All over the world, often long in advance of effective in-
> dustrialization, the unskilled poor are streaming away from
> subsistence agriculture to exchange the squalor of rural
> poverty for the even deeper miseries of the shanty-towns,
> favelas, and bidonvilles that, year by year, grow inexorably
> on the fringes of the developing cities. They . . . are the
> core of local despair and disaffection--filling the Jeunesse
> movements of the Congo, swelling the urban mobs of Rio,
> voting Communist in the ghastly alleys of Calcutta, every-
> where undermining the all too frail structure of public order
> and thus retarding the economic development that alone can
> help their plight.[3]

While the ideological tone and direction are certainly different, the assumptions of these Western economists are not inconsistent with the analysis of Frantz Fanon, who saw a revolutionary role for the urban lumpenproletariat. As Fanon put it:

> The men whom the growing population of the country districts
> and colonial expropriation have brought to desert their
> family holdings circle tirelessly around the different
> towns, hoping that one day or another they will be allowed
> inside. It is within this mass of humanity, this people of
> the shanty-towns, at the core of the lumpen-proletariat
> that the rebellion [against colonialism] will find its urban
> spearhead.[4]

With hindsight, it is possible to see shortcomings in this general model of urban political unrest. Robin Cohen and David Michael, for example, have cogently questioned the evidence on which "Fanonists" base their supposition of a revolutionary

---

[2]Ibid., p. 20.

[3]Quoted in Joan Nelson, Migrants, Urban Poverty, and Instability in Developing Nations (Center for International Affairs, Harvard University: Occasional Papers in International Affairs, No. 22; September 1969), p. 6.

[4]The Wretched of the Earth (Harmondsworth: Penguin, 1967), pp. 102-103.

role for the urban lumpenproletariat in Africa.[5] Their argument
is supported with evidence from Turkey by Ned Levine.[6] In an
extensive study using data from North Africa, Latin America,
and Asia, Joan Nelson persuasively attacks the more simplistic
theories that suggest that radical political action will be
undertaken by the poorest urban migrants.[7] Variations of es-
sentially the same argument have been put forward by Myron
Weiner for India,[8] Wayne A. Cornelius for Mexico,[9] Talton F.
Ray for Venezuela,[10] and Sandra Powell for Peru[11]--to mention
only a few examples. A refined version of the urban radicaliza-
tion hypothesis bypasses a direct role for the lumpenproletariat,
and suggests that "deepening contrasts of affluence and misery
in the cities . . . would radicalize student opinion and stimulate
revolutionary middle-class leadership."[12] If the earlier focus
on the direct revolutionary role of the lumpenproletariat led
policymakers to propose immediate, tangible, but limited improvements in their living conditions in the cities, the more recent

---

[5]"The Revolutionary Potential of the African Lumpenproletariat:
A Sceptical View," Bulletin (University of Sussex, Institute of
Development Studies), Vol. 5, No. 2/3 (October 1973), pp. 31-42.
A more sympathetic approach to Fanon's views on this subject can
be found in Peter Worsley, "Frantz Fanon and the 'Lumpenprole-
tariat'" in Ralph Miliband and John Saville, eds., The Socialist
Register 1972 (London: Merlin Press, 1972), pp. 193-230.

[6]"The Revolutionary Non-Potential of the 'Lumpen': Essence
or Technical Deficiency?," Bulletin, Vol. 5, No. 2/3 (October
1973), pp. 43-52.

[7]Nelson.

[8]"Urbanization and Political Protest," Civilisations, Vol.
17, Nos. 1-2 (1967), pp. 44-52.

[9]"Urbanization as an Agent in Latin American Political Instability: The Case of Mexico," American Political Science
Review, Vol. 63, No. 3 (September 1969), pp. 833-57.

[10]The Politics of the Barrios of Venezuela (Berkeley and Los
Angeles: University of California Press, 1969).

[11]"Political Participation in the Barriadas: A Case Study,"
Comparative Political Studies, Vol. 2, No. 2 (July 1969), pp.
195-215.

[12]Barbara Ward, Lenore d'Anjou, and J.D. Runnalls, eds., The
Widening Gap: Development in the 1970's (New York: Columbia
University Press, 1971), p. 143.

appreciation of the multi-class implications of urban inequality
has suggested a much broader range of measures to reduce overall
inequalities.[13]

B. Squatting as a Social Problem

Squatter areas have traditionally been seen as areas of
social breakdown, delinquency, and alienation. Since most
squatter areas are also "slums" (i.e., areas of substandard
housing), Marshall Clinard's generalizations about slums reflect
the prevailing attitude toward squatters:

> Slums vary from one type to another, but certain general pat-
> terns of slum life are universal. Although the slum is
> characterized by inadequate housing, deficient facilities,
> overcrowding, and congestion, it involves much more than
> these elements. Sociologically it is a way of life, a sub-
> culture with a set of norms and values, which is reflected
> in poor sanitation and health practices, deviant behavior,
> and characteristic attributes of apathy and social isolation.
> People who live in slum areas are isolated from the general
> power structures and are regarded as inferior, and slum
> dwellers, in turn, harbor suspicions of the outside world.[14]

An extreme example of the assumed connection between living conditions and social organization is provided in this description
of a squatter settlement in Colombia:

> It is the rudest kind of slum, clustering like a dirty bee-
> hive around the edges of any principal city in Latin
> America. . . . Living almost like animals, the tugurio's
> residents are overwhelmed by animality. Religion, social
> control, education, domestic life are warped and disfigured.[15]

Even sophisticated scholars have taken up the "disease" image
of slum and squatter communities, all too readily assuming that
these areas are socially disorganized, their people the rejects
of progress. Thus, for Daniel Lerner, "the flooding of great
urban centres by people who have no work there" is evidence of

---

[13] Ibid., pp. 143-47.

[14] Slums and Community Development: Experiments in Self-Help
(New York: The Free Press, 1966), p. 3.

[15] Quoted in William Mangin, "Latin American Squatter Settlements: A Problem and a Solution," Latin American Research
Review, Summer 1967, pp. 66-67.

"the contemporary decoupling of the twin processes of urbanisation and industrialisation," as well as that "the modernisation of most of the world is going badly."[16] In support of this conclusion he says:

> Every student of development is aware of the global spread of urban slums--from the _ranchos_ of Caracas and _favellas_ of Rio, to the _gecekondu_ of Ankara, to the _bidonvilles_ and "tin can cities" that infest the metropolitan centres of every developing country from Cairo to Manila.
> The point that must be stressed in referring to this suffering mass of humanity, displaced from the rural areas to the filthy peripheries of the great cities, is that few of them experience the "transition" from agricultural to urban-industrial labour called for by the mechanism of development and the model of modernisation. They are neither housed, nor trained, nor employed, nor serviced. They languish on the urban periphery without entering into any productive relationship with its industrial operations. These are the "displaced persons," the DPs, of the developmental process as it now typically occurs in most of the world, a human flotsam and jetsam that has been displaced from traditional agricultural life without being incorporated into modern industrial life.[17]

Since the 1960's, most writers have rejected the view that squatter areas are characterized by disorganization, antisocial activities, and crime, and serve no meaningful social purpose. On the basis of their work in Lima, John Turner and William Mangin argue that squatter settlements in Latin America are "solutions to difficult problems rather than . . . problems in themselves"; squatter settlements are "a process of social reconstruction through popular initiative."[18] As I have noted elsewhere, sociologists and anthropologists working in Africa have consistently seen purpose, organization, and community in urban slums.[19] A recent lengthy study of a squatter village in Nairobi comes to the following conclusion:

---

[16]"Comparative Analysis of Processes of Modernisation" in Horace Miner, ed., The City in Modern Africa (London: Pall Mall Press, 1967), p. 25.

[17]_Ibid_., p. 24.

[18]Mangin, p. 67.

[19]Richard Stren, "Urban Policy in Africa: A Political Analysis," African Studies Review, Vol. 15, No. 3 (December 1972), pp. 489-516. A good example is Regina Solzbacher, "East Africa's

Mathare Valley Village 2 is a relatively well-integrated
political community in which residents share a sense of
community and a set of community-wide political institutions which help to provide orderly management and peaceful
resolutions of political and social problems.[20]

Broadly similar findings have been reported by T.G. McGee in a
study of a Malay squatter settlement,[21] and in studies of slum
and squatter communities in Manila.[22]

The policy response to this reorientation in thinking
about low-income settlements has been to move away from demolition and resettlement toward community development and
rehabilitation or improvement of existing squatter areas. Where
possible, these programs are planned in consultation with existing organizations and leadership in the communities themselves.[23]
Even in areas where new low-cost housing is to be built, the
new planning orthodoxy proposes to take into account, and to
use to the maximum, the social and economic resources of the
local population.[24]

Slum Problem: A Question of Definition" in Josef Gugler, ed.,
Urban Growth in Subsaharan Africa (Kampala: Makerere University, 1969 [?]), pp. 45-52.

[20] Marc Ross, The Political Integration of Urban Squatters
(Evanston: Northwestern University Press, 1973), p. 192.

[21] The Southeast Asian City (London: G. Bell and Sons, 1967),
pp. 160-65.

[22] A summary of these studies can be found in Aprodicio A.
Laquian, Rural-Urban Migrants and Metropolitan Development
(Toronto: Methuen Publications for INTERMET, 1971), pp. 145-46.
To quote one passage: "Squatters and slum-dwellers [in Manila]
are very organized, with more than 65 per cent of household
heads being members of at least one organization. Membership
provides not only a sense of community identity but political
power as well" (p. 146).

[23] See, for example, Colin Rosser, "Action Planning in Calcutta:
The Problem of Community Participation," Journal of Development
Studies, Vol. 8, No. 3 (April 1972), pp. 121-39.

[24] These approaches are spelled out in detail in two United
Nations documents: Manual on Self-Help Housing (1964) ST/SOA/53,
and Social Aspects of Housing and Urban Development (1967)
ST/SOA/71.

C. Squatting as an Economic Problem

Squatting is mainly a reflection of two economic factors:
(1) shortages in socially acceptable housing and (2) shortages
in formal employment opportunities. We shall discuss each of
these in turn.

Housing. It is generally accepted that one of the major
reasons for squatting and overcrowded slums is the shortfall
between housing need and demand, on the one hand, and housing
supply, on the other. As John Turner has put it: "Autonomous
urban settlement . . . is the product of the difference between
the nature of the popular demand for dwellings and those supplied
by institutionalized society."[25] The ability of new urban
migrants to pay for minimal standard permanent housing is limited;
as a result, though the need for housing increases very rapidly,
the effective demand is too low to induce a large increase in
housing supply which meets publicly accepted standards. Until
lower-class incomes rise very substantially in comparison to
costs of construction (an unlikely prospect in the near future),
the shortfall in low-cost permanent housing will increase.
Since people have to live somewhere, squatting and serious over-
crowding of low-rental dwellings (slums) will proliferate.

A common response to the problem, as it is perceived in
terms of the sectoral demand-supply model, has been to set up
a national housing agency to build large numbers of low-cost
units. While some of these agencies have been innovative, by
and large they have failed to meet their construction targets
and have built at standards or in locations which put their
housing out of the range of most lower-income groups. There
have been many documented cases where public housing agencies
have demolished slums in order to replace them with modern
buildings, but the former slum residents have been unable to
afford the rents in the new dwellings.[26] The emphasis by some
governments on the public construction of conventional housing
units as a major index of progress has led to what is called
the "product" approach to housing. This "product" approach has
had its most notable successes in cities with a high level of

---

[25]John F.C. Turner, "Uncontrolled Urban Settlement: Problems
and Policies" in Gerald Breese, ed., The City in Newly Developing
Countries (Englewood Cliffs: Prentice-Hall, 1969), p. 511.

[26]For examples, see Peter Marris, Family and Social Change
in an African City (Evanston: Northwestern University Press,
1961), esp. ch. 8, and Frederick Temple, "Politics, Planning
and Housing Policy in Nairobi" (unpublished dissertation, M.I.T.,
1973), pp. 330-39.

economic development and limited land resources, such as Singapore and Hong Kong. But it was also an aspect of the "leading sector strategy" adopted in the 1971-74 Colombian Plan.[27]

Employment. As the larger Third World cities grow in size, employment opportunities in modern or large-scale establishments do not increase at the same rate. "The result," says one observer, "has been either unemployment or under-employment in small-scale, often individual or family-run, establishments."[28] It is often assumed that the highest rates of unemployment are among the more recent urban migrants,[29] and that disproportionate numbers of recent migrants live in slums and squatter areas.[30] Whatever the distinctions between migrants and non-migrants, the general trend is for those with low incomes and irregular wages to gravitate to areas which have the lowest rents or housing costs, are close to employment (or opportunities for casual employment), and are relatively free of legal controls.[31]

---

[27] Lauchlin Currie, "The Colombian Plan 1971-1974: A Test of the Leading Sector Strategy," World Development, Vol. 2, Nos. 10-12 (October/December 1974), pp. 69-72. The two leading sectors in the plan were exports and construction.

[28] C.R. Frank, Jr., "Urban Unemployment and Economic Growth in Africa," Oxford Economic Papers (New Series), Vol. 20 (July 1968), p. 250.

[29] Henry Rempel, "Labor Migration into Urban Centers and Urban Unemployment in Kenya" (unpublished dissertation, University of Wisconsin, 1971), p. 7.

[30] An example of the tendency to associate slum or squatter areas with recent migrants is IDRC and INTERMET, Town Drift: Social and Policy Implications of Rural-Urban Migration in Eight Developing Countries (Ottawa, 1973), ch. 4.

[31] A study of unemployment in Uganda, for example, showed that "little over a quarter of the unemployed were actually living in the housing estates or company housing in the urban areas, while nearly half were living in villages round the towns, quite a few of which were more than five miles from the town centre. In Kampala a large proportion (40 per cent of the Kampala group) were living in the unplanned areas of Mengo where it is common for landlords to erect rows of rented rooms for hire to immigrant workers. A similar pattern is found in the villages nearest to Jinja where dense complexes of rental buildings house immigrant commuters" (Caroline Hutton, Reluctant Farmers? A Study of Unemployment and Planned Rural Development in Uganda (Nairobi: East African Publishing House, 1973), pp. 54-55.

Many administrative officials and politicians see a direct link between unemployment and crime, and treat squatter areas as if they are a threat to national security. In 1972 a speech by President Kenyatta in Nairobi was reported as follows:

> Vagrants and idlers in Nairobi and other towns throughout Kenya were yesterday reminded by President Kenyatta of his call to "go back to the land" to help the farming community continue developing the country. . . . "Our country has no place for lazy and idle people," he said. . . . "Those who believe in hanging around Nairobi and other towns must heed my call of 'go back to the land.' It is only when we have got rid of vagrants and idlers that we can eradicate robbery and thefts," the President said.[32]

Later the same year, statements made by the President's senior administrative official for Nairobi in justifying the demolition of some squatter dwellings in the city were reported thus:

> [He] said shanties were harbouring hundreds of criminals. Many of them are often responsible for pick-pocketing incidents and night-time robberies, he alleged.
> [He] warned that the law would not tolerate such activities and war had been declared to deal with such culprits, he said. The shanty dwellers were unwanted as the structures they had were illegal and a danger to the peaceful and law-abiding citizens of the city.
> Mr. Mburu said all those living in the shanties had their homes, and even land, back in the reserves but did not wish to stay there. "The Government, therefore, has no alternative but to take them back to their homes," he said.[33]

What this analysis by the Kenya elite seems to overlook is (as John R. Harris and Michael P. Todaro have argued) that urban unemployment may be a rational economic response to certain conditions.[34] Harris and Todaro suggest that rural-urban migration may be conditioned not only by actual employment openings in the wage economy, but also by the discounted possibility of finding urban employment in the future. The higher the wage differential between rural and urban employment (however difficult this may be to measure),[35] the greater the flow of rural-urban

---

[32]East African Standard (Nairobi), 28 September 1972.

[33]Daily Nation (Nairobi), 1 December 1972.

[34]"Migration, Unemployment and Development: A Two-Sector Analysis," The American Economic Review, Vol. 60, No. 1, pp. 126-42.

[35]In an excellent survey of the literature on African migration,

migrants and the longer individuals will be prepared to remain in the cities without employment. While the Harris-Todaro model has not yet been rigorously tested,[36] to the extent that it is valid, governments would have to take a number of integrated measures to reduce urban unemployment. In addition to accelerating labor-intensive industrial output, governments would be well-advised to eliminate urban-rural wage differentials through comprehensive incomes policies, and undertake intensive agricultural and rural development.[37] The employment problem represented by squatter areas would thus become a target for a national planning strategy.

An alternative approach to the urban employment problem focuses on the nature of urban employment rather than the dynamics of migration. Thus, following the tradition of Third World "dual

---

Derek Byerlee discusses the enormous difficulties of arriving at accurate measurements for urban and rural wages at a given point in time: "Even if measures of rural and urban incomes are obtained, there are several difficulties in comparing the two. Firstly, because there are larger numbers of educated people in urban areas a comparison of average rural and urban incomes must adjust for the educational composition of the population. Second, the urban worker does not consume all his income since some is shared among the unemployed and remitted to rural areas. Third, there are various problems of conversion to real incomes where prices are higher but social amenities are more available in urban areas. Finally, the relevant variable is not the actual income differential but the differential perceived by potential migrants in rural areas. Lack of information on urban employment opportunities may be one reason for differences in actual and perceived incomes, but the formation of income expectations is likely to be a complex interaction of education, age and aspirations" (Research on Migration in Africa: Past Present and Future [African Rural Employment Study: Rural Employment Paper No. 2; Department of Agricultural Economics, Michigan State University, September 1972], p. 10).

[36] Ibid., p. 9. The same point is also made in Derek Byerlee and Carl K. Eicher, Rural Employment, Migration and Economic Development: Theoretical Issues and Empirical Evidence from Africa (African Rural Employment Study: Rural Employment Paper No. 1; Department of Agricultural Economics, Michigan State University, September 1972), p. 24.

[37] Todaro, "Income Expectations, Rural-Urban Migration and Employment in Africa" in Employment in Africa: Some Critical Issues (Geneva: International Labour Office, 1973), pp. 43-69.

economy" models,[38] an International Labour Office (ILO) report
on Kenya distinguishes between the "formal" and the "informal"
sectors in urban areas.[39] While the informal sector as such is
not precisely defined,

> . . . informal activities are the way of doing things,
> characterised by -- (a) ease of entry; (b) reliance on
> indigenous resources; (c) family ownership of enterprises;
> (d) small scale of operation; (e) labour-intensive and
> adapted technology; (f) skills acquired outside the formal
> school system; and (g) unregulated and competitive markets.[40]

In attempting to estimate the magnitude of unemployment in the
informal sector in Nairobi, the ILO study relies heavily on data
for squatter settlements--"for it is in the squatter areas that
we would expect to find the highest rates of unemployment."[41]

Among the policies recommended by the ILO to promote
the urban informal sector in Kenya are the abandonment of a
slum demolition policy, drastic alterations in trade licensing
policies, the encouragement through loans and research of small-
scale enterprises and technology, and a lowering of high government standards for goods and services which can only be applied
effectively to the minority in the formal sector.[42] With some
reservations, the Kenya government has accepted these recommendations in principle.[43]

---

[38]Illustrative readings on this theme have been collected in
Gerald M. Meier, ed., Leading Issues in Development Economics
(New York: Oxford University Press, 1964), pp. 48-89.

[39]A useful survey of the ILO country studies on employment
can be found in Erik Thorbecke, "The Employment Problem: A
Critical Evaluation of Four ILO Comprehensive Country Reports,"
International Labour Review (1973), pp. 393-423. Of the four
reports evaluated, the Kenya report has the most developed ideas
on the "informal sector."

[40]Employment, Incomes and Equality: A Strategy for Increasing
Productive Employment in Kenya (Geneva: International Labour
Office, 1972), p. 6.

[41]Ibid., p. 55.

[42]Ibid., ch. 13.

[43]Republic of Kenya. Sessional Paper on Employment No. 10 of
1973 (Nairobi: Government Printer, 1973), pp. 44-46.

The ILO approach to urban employment is among the most innovative yet presented, but some commentators have expressed reservations about the extent to which the Kenya elite can be expected to carry out proposals the government has agreed to on paper. This problem is recognized by the leaders of the Kenya ILO mission, who in a revealing postscript write:

> The real issue is, of course, the political feasibility of the strategy proposed. Already the post-independence structures of incomes and land ownership, power and position, have become more firmly based, though the patterns of privilege and class are still affected by traditional family and other ties. Local interests are bound in important ways to interests abroad through the links of trade and private investment, particularly as regards the developed countries. This constellation of local and overseas interests, of which there are many but not all of which are concordant, makes it difficult to effect the change of strategy required.[44]

Two political scientists have pointed to shortcomings of this strategy. Herbert Werlin questions whether policies designed to help Nairobi's squatters and unlicensed traders can ever be effectively implemented in a political system in which disadvantaged groups do not organize to promote their interests.[45] Colin Leys contends that the ILO proposals look only to "the possibility of a reformed capitalism, free from contradictions," rather than to a fundamental change in the system.[46] For Leys, the informal sector "denotes primarily a system of very intense exploitation of labour, with very low wages and often very long hours, underpinned by the constant pressure for work from the 'reserve army' of job seekers."[47] The informal sector thus indirectly serves important and politically powerful interests in the formal sector. Leys concludes that the ILO proposals would at best probably only reinforce the existing socioeconomic system:

---

[44] Hans Singer and Richard Jolly, "Unemployment in an African Setting: Lessons of the Employment Strategy Mission to Kenya" in Employment in Africa . . ., p. 105.

[45] "The Informal Sector: The Implications of the ILO's Study of Kenya," African Studies Review, Vol. 17, No. 1 (April 1974), pp. 205-12.

[46] "Interpreting African Underdevelopment: Reflections on the ILO Report on Employment, Incomes and Equality in Kenya," African Affairs, Vol. 72 (October 1973), p. 428.

[47] Ibid., p. 426.

The most probable effect of the mission's proposals--even
in the unlikely event of its recommendations on income
redistribution and the circumscription of foreign capital
being implemented--would be primarily to direct business
to low-wage African-owned enterprises, and to enable a new
stratum of the African petty-bourgeoisie to transcend the
limitations of the competitive market and achieve a measure
of protection among the ranks of the auxiliary bourgeoisie.[48]

Leys' analysis of the Kenya case parallels a set of
proposals by John Friedmann and Flora Sullivan for absorbing more
urban labor in developing countries.[49] After a brief review of
the material concerning spreading squatter areas, poor urban
services, and increasing migration in relation to urban employment available, Friedmann and Sullivan construct a model of the
urban employment market from which three major hypotheses are
drawn: (1) the poorest employment sectors of the urban economy
will continue to grow; (2) any improvement in services to, or
income for, these sectors will be absorbed by additional rural
immigration; and (3) the equilibrium point for these sectors
will continue to be absolute subsistence. They continue:

> In a situation such as this, marked by extreme and steadily
> increasing forms of inequality, governments have essentially
> two options: either to side with those who wield the instru-
> ments of economic power and use repressive measures against
> the poor and their advocates in order to maintain political
> stability, or to assume the active leadership of the mass
> of the population, both rural and urban, and to devise an
> economic system that will achieve continued economic expansion
> together with increased equality in the distribution of the
> product.[50]

To achieve such a new system, Friedmann and Sullivan argue,
Third World governments will have to shift from maximizing growth
in GNP to maximizing human potential, from a system based on
inequality to one of greater equality and social justice, from
foreign dependence to greater national autonomy and self-reliance,
from import-substitution to an explicit policy of industrial
dualism, from planning for urban primacy to balanced rural-urban
development, and from high rates of natural population increase

---

[48]Ibid., pp. 427-28.

[49]"The Absorption of Labor in the Urban Economy: The Case of
Developing Countries," Economic Development and Cultural Change,
Vol. 22, No. 3 (April 1974), pp. 385-413.

[50]Ibid., p. 405.

to a policy based on stabilization. To deal with a specific
urban problem, in short, the authors are led to proposals which--
if fully implemented--would drastically change the economic and
political configurations in most Third World countries.

D. Squatting as a Problem in Physical Planning

Much of the concern about squatter areas in the Third
World derives from the poor physical conditions of the neighborhoods. Evidence from many countries shows the dilapidated
quality of most squatter housing, the overcrowding, the limited
or nonexistent sanitary and recreation facilities, and the lack
of amenities such as water, electricity, and decent roads. At
the same time, planners often feel that land occupied by squatters could be more usefully zoned for other purposes. The
extent to which squatters are able to defy planning regulations
makes the law that much more difficult to apply in other areas.
At the very least, effective planning controls would lead to
improvements in both the quality of housing and the level of
amenities available.

In a number of influential papers, John Turner has presented a forceful case for a different approach to physical
planning.[51] The main reason for unregulated residential growth,
he argues, is the failure of planners (and their governments)
to adjust middle-class standards and values to lower-class needs.
Slum demolition, the principle of requiring "minimum modern
standards" of building before security of tenure can be granted,
and the provision of "instant" dwelling units in permanent
materials by large organizations are all examples of the prevailing middle-class bias. On the basis of his own experience
in Lima, Turner maintains that the expression of lower-class
needs through squatter development is a progressive force in
urbanization. The progressive aspects are shown primarily in
two ways: (1) the close relationship between security of legal
tenure to land and housing and the levels of physical development
in particular settlements;[52] and (2) the improvement in socio-

---

[51]Turner's three most important papers are "Barriers and Chan-
nels for Housing Development in Modernizing Countries," American
Institute of Planners Journal, Vol. 33 (May 1967), pp. 167-81;
"Housing Priorities, Settlement Patterns, and Urban Development
in Modernizing Countries," American Institute of Planners Journal,
Vol. 34 (November 1968), pp. 354-63; and "Uncontrolled Urban
Settlement: Problems and Policies" in Gerald Breese, ed., The
City in Newly Developing Countries (Englewood Cliffs: Prentice-
Hall, 1969).

[52]Turner, "Uncontrolled Urban Settlement . . .," esp. pp. 514-
20.

economic status achieved over time by household heads who begin in slum settlements "seeking a toehold in the urban system."[53] "The basic problem of the slums," Turner says, "is not how to eradicate them, but how to make them livable."[54] Among the changes this new planning strategy would involve are:

> . . . the abandonment of the currently orthodox modern project approach to urban development and the substitution of a service approach. In institutionally and economically underdeveloped societies, the governing class in general and public administrators in particular must give up the idea that they can act unilaterally and effectively on behalf of the mass of the people. Government influence on development will be proportional to its understanding of ordinary people's needs and its ability to work, not for them but with them.[55]

This strategy has stimulated a number of new approaches to planning for lower-income groups. In line with the notion that lower-income housing should serve economic and locational functions rather than meet middle-class construction standards which cost upwards of twice the capital outlay, much more thought is being given to public investment in mass transport, to the upgrading of existing slum areas (with better roads, water, electricity, community facilities, and the like), and to the "sites and services" model of neighborhood growth.[56] There is an apparent paradox in these approaches, however: they imply a much higher and more efficient level of urban administrative infrastructure than exists at present in most developing countries. (Turner's approach, on the other hand, points to a more flexible--even minimal--structure of public administrative controls and agencies.) This paradox strongly suggests that the administrative implications of these new approaches have yet to be worked out in detail for Third World countries in the process of rapid urbanization.

The "popular" approach to physical planning in the Third World, as expressed most clearly by Turner, makes two sweeping assumptions. The first assumption is that economic opportunities for low-income migrants will improve sufficiently that more

---

[53]Turner, "Housing Priorities . . .," p. 358.

[54]Turner, "Uncontrolled Urban Settlement . . .," p. 526.

[55]Turner, "Housing Priorities . . .," p. 362.

[56]See, for example, the programs presented in The World Bank, Urbanization: Sector Working Paper.

flexible planning arrangements will aid the migrant in establishing himself. Given security of tenure and less stringent building regulations, houseowners should improve their living standard over time, plowing income back into progressive residential improvements. While this developmental sequence may well have described Lima into the mid-1960's, even Turner admits that it is not an adequate description of, for example, urban processes in Calcutta.[57] At a minimum, economic opportunities would have to be continually expanding, and urban household heads would have to be prepared to invest their surplus funds almost exclusively in urban, rather than rural, property. Neither of these conditions is likely to be met in many of the poorer states of contemporary Asia and Africa.

The second assumption of the new, "popular" approach is that planners and their governments will be prepared to carry out the prescribed changes. The present system as Turner describes it--where the "progressive development" of slums and squatter areas is inhibited by a maze of government regulations and the "middle-class values" of the planners--can be shown to serve the interests of the governing elite. Assuming that the amount of resources available for urban development remains constant, Turner's approach, which calls for more infrastructural investment and increased availability of loan funds for the lower-income areas, would be to the relative disadvantage of the commercial and residential areas where the governing elite presently work and live. Such a shift in urban investment priorities could only come about as a result of a political realignment which would give the poor vastly more influence over the allocation of resources than they appear to have at present. There is already considerable evidence of powerful local elites gaining control of international aid projects which were originally intended to benefit lower-income groups. Whether the support given to the interests of the poor by international development agencies will be sufficient to overcome their lack of domestic power will be a key question in the 1970's.

The preceding discussion of urban squatting in terms of its political, social, economic, and physical aspects is intended to show that squatting cannot be viewed as an isolated malfunction of society that can be dealt with by limited means, independent of other considerations. While both structural-functionalists and Marxists would probably agree on this minimal proposition, there is considerable disagreement concerning the extent of change necessary in societies and their mechanisms of economic

---

[57]Turner, "Housing Priorities . . .," p. 358.

allocation before the present bifurcated pattern of urbanization in the Third World is substantially modified. At the very
least, however, even the more conservative planners would urge
a government desirous of diminishing the growth of urban squatting
to reduce urban-rural wage differences, to decentralize development away from the largest cities, and to limit income dispar-
ities within the cities themselves. In Tanzania, such policies
have been adopted, but the country still has a very significant
and growing squatter population. A consideration of why this
is so will point up some of the problems of planning for socialism
in a poor country.

The analysis that follows is divided into three major
sections. In Chapter II the pattern of urbanization in Tanzania
is described and the development of a national urban policy
outlined. In Chapter III the squatter "problem" in the aggregate
is analyzed, and some reasons suggested for its growth in importance in recent years. In Chapter IV some survey data on
the characteristics of both squatters and non-squatters in Dar
es Salaam are presented in order to bring out some of the
salient dimensions of urban inequality reflected in the squatting
phenomenon. In the concluding chapter it is suggested that both
some rather narrow "technical" solutions and some broad structural changes will be necessary to alleviate the problems posed
by squatting.

Chapter II

URBAN GROWTH AND URBAN POLICY IN TANZANIA

A. Urban Growth in Mainland Tanzania

        Urban patterns in mainland Tanzania today are largely
a product of the colonial period and its aftermath. Some important towns arose before German colonization as a result of
coastal trade with Arabia and India, trade with the Portuguese,
and the slave trade. But most of them (with the exception of
Tabora and Kigoma/Ujiji) were on the coast and are no longer
prominent. The coastal town of Bagamoyo, for example, which
prospered during the early part of the nineteenth century as a
link between Indian Ocean commerce and the African continental
trade, declined markedly when German rule was imposed in the
1880's.[1] It was almost completely eclipsed by the development
of Dar es Salaam as the colonial administrative and commercial
center. "The major influence of the ancient towns," says Adolfo
Mascarenhas, "was the evolution and dissemination of the Swahili
language and to a minor extent the spread of Islam."[2]

        Two of the most significant features of urbanization in
twentieth-century mainland Tanzania are (1) that the country's
population has remained overwhelmingly rural and (2) the disproportionate growth of the capital city. In 1948 there were
four urban areas with a population in excess of 10,000; in 1957
there were eleven in this category; by 1967 there were only
fourteen. As a proportion of the total population, these urban
areas comprised 1.5 percent in 1948, 3.3 percent in 1957, and
5.0 percent in 1967.[3] According to Economic Commission for
Africa estimates, only six of the 35 sub-Saharan countries had
proportionately smaller urban populations in 1970.[4] In the

---

[1]Walter T. Brown, "Bagamoyo: An Historical Introduction,"
Tanzania Notes and Records, 71 (1970), pp. 69-83.

[2]"Urban Centres" in L. Berry, ed., Tanzania in Maps (London:
University of London Press, 1971), p. 130.

[3]These calculations are made from data in Tanzania, Statistical
Abstract 1966 and Statistical Abstract 1970 (Dar es Salaam:
Government Printer, 1968 and 1972).

[4]Colin Rosser, Urbanization in Tropical Africa: A Demographic

least urbanized continent in the world, Tanzania is one of the
least urbanized countries. At the same time, the urban areas
in the aggregate are growing substantially faster than the rural
population. Between 1948 and 1957, the total urban population
of Tanzania increased annually by 7.1 percent, while the rural
population increased annually by 1.5 percent. From 1957 to
1967, the respective rates of growth were 6.4 percent and 2.9
percent.[5] Over the whole period from 1948 to 1967, the mainland
rural population grew at an average annual compound rate of 2.3
percent, compared to an urban rate of 6.8 percent.[6] Thus the
urban areas have been growing in population at almost three
times the rate of the rural areas. Given the small size of
Tanzania's original urban base, this rapid growth has put tremendous pressure on an already hard-pressed government to provide
employment, services, and amenities for urban residents.

Overall rates of urban growth mask considerable differences between towns, as shown in Table 1. For the mainland
(excluding Zanzibar) Dar es Salaam, with a population of 272,821
in 1967, was more than 4.5 times as large as the second largest
town, Tanga, which had a population of 61,058. Tanga, in turn,
was 1.8 times as large as Mwanza. After Mwanza, the decrease
in size becomes much more gradual. As for growth rates, Dar es
Salaam grew at an average rate of 7.5 percent per annum between
1948 and 1967--somewhat higher than the urban average for the
whole country. While no urban areas lost population, towns like
Tabora, Mtwara, and Lindi grew only slightly more rapidly than
the rural population. In 1967 Dar es Salaam alone had 45.3
percent of the mainland population in towns over 10,000.

The literature on Third World urbanization has often
cited rural-urban migration as the source of the bulk of urban
population increases--particularly within the low-income section
of the population.[7] The Tanzanian data provide evidence to support the first part of this generalization, but suggest modifica-
tion of the second part.

Introduction (New York: Ford Foundation International Urbanization Survey, 1972), p. 15. The six less urbanized countries
were Upper Volta, Mauritania, Portuguese Guinea, Uganda, Burundi,
and Mozambique.

[5]Calculated from Berry, Tanzania in Maps, p. 170.

[6]C.-F. Claeson and B. Egero, Migration and the Urban Population:
A Demographic Analysis of Population Census Data for Tanzania
(University of Dar es Salaam: BRALUP Research Notes No. 11:2,
1972), p. 5.

[7]For example, Laquian, and IDRC and INTERMET, Town Drift.

URBAN GROWTH AND URBAN POLICY IN TANZANIA

Table 1

TANZANIA MAINLAND URBAN POPULATION IN TOWNS OVER 10,000
IN 1967 AND AVERAGE RECORDED GROWTH, 1948-1967

Town	Population, 1967	Average Annual Growth Rate, 1948-1967
Dar es Salaam	272,821	7.5%
Tanga	61,058	5.9
Mwanza	34,861	6.1
Arusha	32,452	10.0
Moshi	26,864	6.5
Morogoro	25,262	6.1
Dodoma	23,559	4.9
Iringa	21,746	7.3
Kigoma/Ujiji	21,369	7.3
Tabora	21,012	2.7
Mtwara/Mikindani	20,413	2.7
Musoma	15,412	9.1
Lindi	13,352	2.4
Mbeya	12,479	7.5
Total mainland urban	610,801	6.8
Total mainland rural	11,347,853	2.3
Total mainland	11,958,654	2.5

Source: Migration and the Urban Population (University of Dar
es Salaam: BRALUP Research Notes No. 11:2, June 1972),
pp. 5-6.

Most of the hard information on the demographic cor-
relates of urban growth in Tanzania comes from analyses of the
most recent (1967) census. In particular, three studies by the
Bureau of Resource Assessment and Land Use Planning (BRALUP) of
the University of Dar es Salaam add significantly to our knowledge
of migration and the demography of urbanization.[8] For the
analysis of migration, the most crucial variable in the 1967
census is place of birth. Since comparable data do not exist
for previous censuses, the picture provided in the BRALUP studies
is static rather than developmental. Fortunately, these data
can be supplemented to give a more dynamic perspective, as we
shall demonstrate.

For urban residents there are five birthplace categories
which may be derived from the 1967 census: (1) same locality
(born in town of residence); (2) same region (born in region
of residence but not in the town); (3) other region (born in
other Tanzanian region); (4) other African country; (5) non-
African country. Table 2 summarizes the birthplace data for all
mainland towns over 10,000 in 1967. Although almost all the
towns (with the exception of Mwanza) had a majority of the population born in the town or region of enumeration, all but
Kigoma/Ujiji showed considerably less than half born in the
town itself. In all mainland towns combined, 65.7 percent were
born outside the towns themselves, and thus can be considered
migrants.[9]

The demographic and socioeconomic characteristics of
migrants in Tanzania have been related to both structural and
attitudinal factors in order to explain rural-urban migration.
During the colonial period, migration to the Tanzanian towns
was mainly a movement of able-bodied young men looking for employment.[10] In Dar es Salaam in the 1930's, John Iliffe suggests, most of the African inhabitants "were presumably target
workers: that is, they visited the town in order to earn a
fixed sum of money which they needed at home."[11] And in the

---

[8]The three studies produced by BRALUP (written by Claes-Fredrik
Claeson and Bertil Egero) are Movement to Towns in Tanzania:
Tables and Comments (Research Notes No. 11:1, 1971), Migration
and the Urban Population: A Demographic Analysis of Population
Census Data for Tanzania (Research Notes No. 11:2, 1972), and
Migration in Tanzania: A Review Based on the 1967 Population
Census (Research Notes No. 11:3, 1972).

[9]BRALUP, Movement to Towns in Tanzania, p. 24.

[10]Mascarenhas, p. 132.

[11]"The Age of Improvement and Differentiation (1907-45)" in

URBAN GROWTH AND URBAN POLICY IN TANZANIA

Table 2

TANZANIA MAINLAND URBAN POPULATION IN TOWNS OVER 10,000
BY BIRTHPLACE CATEGORY: 1967

Town	Birthplace					
	Same Locality	Same Region	Other Region	Other African Country	Non-African Country	
Arusha	30.0%	12.8%	46.0%	7.1%	4.0%	(99.0%)
Dar es Salaam	32.5	23.9	35.2	4.4	4.0	(100.0)
Dodoma	26.9	25.9	41.3	3.5	2.4	(100.0)
Iringa	39.9	35.3	20.7	2.3	1.9	(100.1)
Kigoma/ Ujiji	59.8	18.4	10.7	10.3	0.7	(99.9)
Lindi	31.3	54.4	9.8	2.5	2.5	(100.1)
Mbeya	31.6	33.0	25.8	6.6	3.0	(100.0)
Morogoro	32.0	42.2	21.3	2.5	2.1	(100.1)
Moshi	30.0	31.1	27.2	7.6	3.9	(100.0)
Mtwara/ Mikindani	38.5	44.0	10.5	5.9	1.1	(100.0)
Musoma	27.3	40.9	18.0	11.9	1.9	(100.0)
Mwanza	40.8	3.2	42.8	9.1	4.0	(99.9)
Tabora	40.4	23.4	28.0	5.8	2.4	(100.0)
Tanga	35.3	37.5	19.0	4.5	3.8	(99.9)
All Towns	34.3	26.8	30.2	5.2	3.4	(99.9)

Source: Movement to Towns in Tanzania: Tables and Comments (University of Dar es Salaam: BRALUP Research Notes No. 11:1, April 1971), pp. 24-25.

25

1950's, P.H. Gulliver's study of migrant laborers from Ungoni (a rural area) showed that

> Without question the overwhelming reason why Ngoni leave their homes and their country to seek work abroad is economic. Men cannot, or feel they cannot, earn sufficient money at home to satisfy their basic cash needs and their minimum standard of living; alternatively, men feel that it is easier to earn sufficient abroad than at home.[12]

In the urban areas, this type of migrant was mainly an unskilled worker, says Iliffe, "but the skilled immigrant was also in a sense a target worker, in that his aim was to save sufficient during his career to enable him to enjoy his retirement in his home area."[13] An analysis of the African population of Dar es Salaam written in 1957 suggests that there were other factors besides wages which influenced migration decisions:

> People come to Dar es Salaam not to eat well, or to live in comfort without overcrowding. . . . It is not food or housing that draws, but the hope of acquiring money to get the world's goods (both eyes on the high wages, and a fine disregard for the equally high cost of living), the desire for a brighter life and to a large extent a tradition among many coastal tribes that one must have seen Dar es Salaam to have lived; an escape from the discipline of family, tribe and government into the uncontributing anonymity of town, where one takes what one can get and puts nothing into the kitty, and with any luck gets away with it. At the same time the young man lives, while remaining invisible to the authorities, to shine among his fellows, as it were, to jump the long queue of promotion in the esteem of the community.[14]

Whatever the "push" or "pull" factors related to migration, a predisposition to seek work in the urban areas was enormously increased by exposure to formal Western education. Since those receiving education during the colonial period were

---

I.N. Kimambo and A.J. Temu, eds., A History of Tanzania (Nairobi: East African Publishing House, 1969), p. 144.

[12] Labour Migration in a Rural Economy (Kampala: East African Institute of Social Research, 1955), p. 16.

[13] Iliffe, p. 144.

[14] J.A.K. Leslie, A Survey of Dar es Salaam (London: Oxford University Press, 1963), p. 31.

predominantly Christian males,[15] a religious bias in the migration stream was produced. The colonial economic system of large wage differentials between skilled (primarily clerical) and unskilled occupations, and between urban and peasant sector incomes, strongly influenced the nature of the migration.[16]

Patterns established during the colonial period with respect to rural-urban migration have been modified, but not substantially changed, since Independence in 1961. Analysis of the 1967 census shows a clear relation between migratory status, on the one hand, and age and male:female ("sex") ratios for the mainland urban population, on the other. This is summarized in Table 3 where, in a comparison of the migrant with the non-migrant population, the migrant group shows a much higher male:female ratio for all age groups over 14 years, and a much lower proportion of children.

The overall sex ratios for specific towns, according to migratory category, are broken down in Table 4. This table shows that the migrant populations born in other regions of the country tend to have much higher male:female sex ratios than do the migrant populations born in the region (but not in the town) of enumeration. The segment of the population born in other regions--comprising 28 percent of the total urban population in 1967--appears to be far from having permanent urban roots. There is evidence that the urban male:female sex ratio is declining over time. In Dar es Salaam, for example, the ratio was 141 in 1948, 131 in 1957, and 123 in 1967.[17]

There continues to be a clear relation between level of education and urban migration. Census data from one of the BRALUP studies, presented in Table 5, show unmistakably that levels of education decline with age, that they vary enormously according to sex, and that urban residents have much higher educational levels than rural residents. When age, sex, and urban residence are held constant, migrants from the same region as the town of enumeration have the lowest levels of educational achievement, followed by the urban-born (non-migrants), migrants

---

[15]Tanganyika, African Census Report 1957 (Dar es Salaam: Government Printer, 1963), p. 72.

[16]For an argument along these lines see Richard H. Sabot, "Education, Income Distribution, and Rates of Urban Migration in Tanzania" (University of Dar es Salaam, Economic Research Bureau Paper 72.6, September 1972).

[17]Central Statistical Bureau, Recorded Population Changes, 1948-67 (Dar es Salaam, 1968), p. 7.

Table 3

AGE DISTRIBUTION AND AGE-SPECIFIC SEX RATIOS FOR THE NON-MIGRANT AND THE MIGRANT POPULATIONS IN URBAN TANZANIA: 1967

Sex/Ratios	Age Groups								All Ages
	0-4	5-9	10-14	15-19	20-34	35-49	50-64	65+	
	Non-Migrant Population								
Male	30.8	18.6	11.5	9.1	16.6	8.8	3.1	1.5	100
Female	30.3	18.4	10.6	8.9	18.8	8.1	3.1	1.8	100
Sex ratio - Male:Female	100	99	107	100	87	108	101	83	99
	Migrant Population								
Male	6.3	6.7	6.1	10.9	40.7	20.2	6.3	2.8	100
Female	8.5	10.1	7.2	12.9	39.2	14.0	5.1	3.0	100
Sex ratio - Male:Female	96	87	109	109	135	187	159	123	130

Source: BRALUP, Migration and the Urban Population, p. 16.

28

Table 4

MALE:FEMALE SEX RATIOS BY BIRTHPLACE CATEGORY
IN TOWNS IN MAINLAND TANZANIA: 1967

Town	Same Locality	Same Region	Other Region	Other African Country	Non-African Country	Total
Arusha	106	88	172	137	108	131
Bukoba	97	116	164	148	116	119
Dar es Salaam	103	115	148	136	130	123
Dodoma	98	93	139	150	138	114
Iringa	88	108	130	135	134	104
Kigoma/Ujiji	88	177	115	92	147	104
Lindi	98	109	124	226	87	107
Mbeya	93	88	127	111	123	101
Morogoro	93	110	134	142	148	110
Moshi	106	132	155	130	111	128
Mtwara/ Mikindani	98	126	169	158	138	119
Musoma	91	99	125	133	166	105
Mwanza	99	87	145	122	128	119
Tabora	89	79	132	123	124	99
Tanga	97	115	164	139	159	118
Total mainland urban	99	112	148	131	130	118

Source: BRALUP, Migration and the Urban Population, p. 15.

Table 5

PROPORTIONS OF POPULATION WITHOUT SCHOOL EDUCATION AND WITH HIGHER EDUCATION, BY SEX, AGE GROUP, RESIDENCE, AND BIRTHPLACE IN MAINLAND TANZANIA: 1967a

Residence and Birthplace	No School Education Age Groups				Five Years or More School Education Age Groups			
	10-14	20-24	30-34	40-44	10-14	20-24	30-34	40-44
		Male						
Total mainland rural	43%	46%	58%	68%	12%	20%	13%	9%
Total mainland urban	16	18	29	37	44	57	45	37
Same locality	14	21	34	41	48	55	42	34
Same region	29	29	42	51	28	37	27	20
Other regions	10	10	19	29	49	68	54	42
Other African countries	13	19	23	33	52	63	56	46
Non-African countries	5	10	10	11	80	81	82	78

URBAN GROWTH AND URBAN POLICY IN TANZANIA

Table 5 (continued)

Residence and Birthplace	No School Education				Five Years or More School Education			
	Age Groups				Age Groups			
	10-14	20-24	30-34	40-44	10-14	20-24	30-34	40-44
	Female							
Total mainland rural	57%	79%	90%	94%	7%	4%	2%	1%
Total mainland urban	23	50	66	74	41	27	20	15
Same locality	19	52	72	81	47	28	15	9
Same region	42	66	83	88	23	12	6	4
Other regions	17	35	56	68	44	36	25	17
Other African countries	21	42	50	64	43	42	35	26
Non-African countries	4	9	14	25	83	85	75	57

[a]Explanatory Note: For each line, the two figures within the same educational group together with the figure not included for education 1-4 years add up to 100 percent.

Source: BRALUP, Migration and the Urban Population, p. 19.

from other regions, migrants from other African countries, and
migrants from non-African countries respectively.

More recent data for Tanzanian urban centers were collected in 1971 by the National Urban Mobility, Employment and
Income Survey of Tanzania (NUMEIST), organized by Manfred
Bienefeld and Richard Sabot of the Economic Research Bureau of
the University of Dar es Salaam. The survey consisted of detailed
interview schedules administered to about 5,500 randomly selected
adults in Dar es Salaam and six other major towns.[18] In Volume
II of the NUMEIST findings, Sabot analyzes the data for urban
migrants. For this analysis, a respondent was classified as a
"migrant" if he had been born outside the town where he was
interviewed and had not come to the town until the age of 14
or older.[19] Thus the migrant population in this survey repre-
sents a statistically different group than the migrant population
as defined in the 1967 census, although there is undoubtedly
considerable overlap. The assumption underlying the 1971 survey
was that anyone 14 years of age or older who migrates to a city
has (at least to some extent) shown the capacity to make independent decisions, and therefore can be directly affected by
government policies. According to the survey, 67 percent of
the respondents were "migrants." Of the remainder, 16 percent
were born in the town where interviewed, and 16 percent had
arrived in town when they were 13 years of age or younger.[20]

The NUMEIST data are too complex and extensive to be
summarized here.[21] (These data will be referred to again in
Chapter IV below.) In the present context, however, it is worth
pointing out the relationship between education and migration
shown in the data.[22] The data show that having an education
is even more of a prerequisite for urban migration now than it

---

[18] The six other towns were Tanga, Arusha, Mwanza, Tabora,
Dodoma, and Mbeya.

[19] R.H. Sabot, Urban Migration in Tanzania (The National Urban
Mobility, Employment and Income Survey of Tanzania, Volume
II; University of Dar es Salaam: Economic Research Bureau,
1972), p. 7.

[20] Ibid., p. 23.

[21] The volume on urban migration has been summarized in some
tables in Appendix I of Annual Manpower Report to the President
1971 (Dar es Salaam: Ministry of Economic Affairs and Development
Planning, Manpower Planning Division, n.d.).

[22] This relationship is explored in Sabot, Urban Migration . . .,
ch. 3.

was in the past. This is to be expected, since the educational
requirements for obtaining urban employment have risen tremen-
dously over the past two decades. Of the migrant males who
arrived in town prior to 1953, 40 percent had no education,
while 32 percent had 5-8 years or more. The proportion of those
with no education has declined steadily with each successive
year of arrival in town, to the point that only 14 percent of
the migrants arriving in 1971 had no education, while 66 percent
had 5-8 years or more. Survey data analyzed by Rempel and Todaro
for Kenya show a similar trend: older urban migrants tend to
have less formal schooling.[23] The Tanzanian data show further
that the higher the level of education, the higher the proportion of migrants who come to town for prearranged employment--
rather than on speculation or with plans for self-employment.
Education is also partly responsible for a recent dramatic shift
in the sex composition of the migrant stream--i.e., "a majority
of the most recent arrivals to both Dar es Salaam and the regional centers are now women." Not only have work opportunities for
educated women increased, but more men are bringing their families
to town--"a phenomenon associated with the rise in wages and
the stabilization of the urban labour force."[24]

Increased stabilization of both employment and urban
residence are related to continuing rural ties. As Josef Gugler
puts it:

Urban residents [in Africa] continue to care about the
opinion people back home hold of them. . . . They derive
emotional security from the firm roots they maintain in
their place of origin while settling down for a working
life in town.[25]

The Tanzanian survey data[26] reflect the pattern found elsewhere
in Africa where workers are spending longer proportions of their

---

[23]H. Rempel and M.P. Todaro, "Rural-to-Urban Labour Migration
in Kenya" in S.H. Ominde and C.N. Ejiogu, eds., Population Growth
and Economic Development in Africa (London: Heinemann, 1972),
p. 225.

[24]Sabot, p. 41.

[25]"On the Theory of Rural-Urban Migration: The Case of Sub-
saharan Africa" in J.A. Jackson, ed., Migration (Sociological
Studies: 2; Cambridge: Cambridge University Press, 1969), p.
149.

[26]Sabot, ch. 8.

working lives in the cities.[27] At the same time, however, access
to land in the rural areas, combined with inadequate social
security arrangements in the city for old people who can no
longer work for wages, has meant that important links with the
rural areas have generally been maintained throughout urban
working careers.[28]

The analysis of the Tanzanian urban wage labor force by
Bienefeld supports this picture of increasing stabilization.
Bienefeld's data (drawn from the NUMEIST survey), which include
both the employed and the self-employed, show that "one in every
three regular wage earners has been in his present job for more
than five years, and half have been there for more than three
years."[29] His analysis leads him to the conclusion that "Tanzania's urban wage earners cluster around a large stable core,
whose stability at work implies stability in terms of urban
residence."[30] Thus, he argues, "the days of short term or
'circular' migrant labour have truly passed in Tanzania's urban
areas, at least for those who are able to obtain wage employment."[31] The "stable core" that Bienefeld points to is becoming
more and more educated, which probably accounts for the rather
startling lack of significant wage-income differences between
migrants and non-migrants.[32] Fewer migrants than non-migrants
are in non-wage employment, and fewer migrants are looking for
work.[33] These findings run significantly counter to the view
that rural-urban migration is a primary cause of urban unemployment and of the growth of the unregulated "informal" sector.

---

[27]See, for example, Walter Elkan, "Is a Proletariat Emerging
in Nairobi?" (University of Nairobi: Institute for Development
Studies, Discussion Paper, 1972).

[28]Sabot, ch. 9.

[29]M.A. Bienefeld, The Wage Employed (The National Urban Mobility, Employment and Income Survey of Tanzania, Volume III;
University of Dar es Salaam: Economic Research Bureau, 1972),
p. 157.

[30]Ibid., p. 160.

[31]Ibid., p. 167.

[32]Ibid., p. 116.

[33]This is partly explained by the fact that the comparatively
affluent Asian population (13 percent of the non-migrant population and 7 percent of the migrant population) were heavily engaged
in non-wage employment.

B. Urban Policy and Performance in Tanzania[34]

In order to check the disproportionate growth of its towns (particularly Dar es Salaam), and to control the form and quality of development within the towns, Tanzania has evolved a set of urban policies consistent with its broad economic and political strategy. An important measure of the adequacy of these policies--in terms of both their substance and their implementation--is the degree to which suitable accommodation and an acceptable level of residential services can be provided for low-income groups. In this section we will analyze and evaluate Tanzania's urban policies with particular attention to their effects on low-income groups.

(1) The Substance of Urban Policy. Until the late 1960's Tanzania had, like most other countries, a patchwork of policies to deal with its growing urban problems. This was partly a legacy of the colonial period and partly a result of the fact that the government considered that its most important challenges lay elsewhere.

With the few exceptions noted above (p. 21), urban development in mainland Tanzania did not begin until the colonial period. During much of the colonial era, Asians, Arabs, and Europeans were considered the "permanent" residents of the towns, while Africans (on the whole) were considered "temporary" workers who would (and should) eventually return to the rural areas. As in other colonies, this attitude toward Africans was partly a justification for their "highly unsatisfactory and shameful housing conditions,"[35] but it also reflected a fear among colonial administrators of the consequences of the development of a class-conscious urban labor force.[36] For these reasons, and because Africans were by far the poorest group in a racially stratified urban society, different housing provisions had to be made for Africans. For example, Township Rules formulated in the 1920's divided urban land into four major zones: (1) a

---

[34] A shorter version of this section can be found in my article "Urban Policy and Performance in Kenya and Tanzania," *Journal of Modern African Studies*, Vol. 13, No. 2 (June 1975).

[35] Aidan Southall, "The Impact of Imperialism upon Urban Development in Africa" in Victor Turner, ed., *Colonialism in Africa 1870-1960*, Vol. III (Cambridge: Cambridge University Press, 1971), p. 246.

[36] Peter C.W. Gutkind, *The Emergent African Urban Proletariat* (Montreal: McGill University, Centre for Developing-Area Studies; Occasional Paper No. 8, 1974), esp. pp. 37-49.

residential zone for Europeans. (2) a commercial/residential
zone for Asians, (3) a residential zone for Africans, and (4) an
industrial zone.[37] Later, town planning was applied on a more
systematic basis through the Town Development Control Ordinance
of 1936, followed by the Town and Country Planning Ordinance
which came into force in 1956. These ordinances were derived
from British town planning legislation; similarly the 1956
building code for Dar es Salaam (in force at least until the
end of 1973) was adapted from the 1927 London Building Act.[38]
The policy under these ordinances was to divide the towns--for
residential purposes--into low-density, medium-density, and
high-density areas. The density classifications determined the
size of housing plots in each area, the level of physical development required per plot, and the standard of services that
would be provided.

Almost all urban Africans lived in the high-density
areas, where plot sizes varied from about 2,500-4,5000 square
feet. Occupancy was generally permitted only on a short-term
basis, while the construction standards were very low. In the
medium-density areas, plots ranged in size from 8,000 square
feet to half an acre; some Africans who could afford more expensive houses obtained smaller plots in these areas in municipal
layouts. In the low-density areas, plot sizes averaged an acre
each, occupancy was usually long-term, and costly building
covenants were contained in property leases with the government,
specifying the value of physical development required. The
provision of facilities was also determined by race/income
considerations:

> In the provision of community facilities, the criterion
> was the ability to pay. Thus the provision of expensive
> facilities such as tarmac roads and sewers was financed
> indirectly through road frontage premia. Thus only the high
> and middle income residential areas, which were synonymous
> with low and medium density residential zones, enjoyed such
> facilities. In the high density residential zones where
> the low income groups lived only dirt roads could be pro-
> vided. Despite high densities per acre as compared to medium

---

[37] J. Mkama, "Urban Development Policies and Planning Experience
in Tanzania" in Michael Safier, ed., The Role of Urban and
Regional Planning in National Development of East Africa (Kampala:
Milton Obote Foundation, 1970), p. 200.

[38] John Leaning, "Housing and Land Distribution in Tanzania"
(Dar es Salaam: Ministry of Lands, Housing and Urban Development,
1971), p. 10.

and low density residential zones, only primitive and less costly forms of sanitation were provided.[39]

After World War II, African immigration to Dar es Salaam and some other towns began to outstrip the rate at which houses were being built privately in the high-density areas. "Shanty towns" began to appear on both public and freehold land. As a result, provision was made in the Ten-Year Development Plan of 1946 for £300,000 for African urban housing; this was raised to £1,230,000 in the Revised Development Plan of 1951. As of 1957 a total of 3,600 houses had been built by the government for rental under the African Urban Housing Scheme.[40] By 1962, 4,389 houses had been built and were being administered by local authorities. At the same time, new areas had been surveyed to enable individual Africans to build traditional houses of their own.

By the mid-1950's, the policy trend in all the East African territories was to further integrate Africans into town life. As the influential East Africa Royal Commission 1953-1955 Report (presented to the British Parliament in June 1955) put it:

The towns are the centres of social and intellectual life, of economic enterprise and of political activity. It is essential to break down the barriers which prevent Africans from full participation in the life of the towns. The African must come to regard the towns as places which fully provide him with an outlet for his courage, ability and initiative.[41]

A Tanganyikan government study, commissioned after the British 1953-1955 report was made public, pointed out an important contradiction in official policy. On the one hand, the government seems to have been committed "to encourage the formation of a stable and contented urban middle class African populace" and to "securing peace and contentment amongst the African urban population."[42] On the other hand, the government had done little in terms of town planning to change the nature of African

---

[39]Mkama, p. 197.

[40]M.J.B. Molohan, Detribalization (Dar es Salaam: Government Printer, 1959), p. 44.

[41]Great Britain, East Africa Royal Commission 1953-1955 Report, Cmd 9475 (London: H.M.S.O., 1961 ed.), p. 250.

[42]Molohan, pp. 44-45.

urban life in Tanganyika. No scheme of tenant-purchase housing--
a mainstay of urban stabilization policy in Kenya--had yet been
instituted. And in the high-density areas in general,

> the provision of services . . . did not keep pace with the
> rate of construction and in many areas proper roads, drainage
> and water supplies were sadly lacking, as also were schools,
> dispensaries and clinics, markets and the like. It is in
> this respect that development of the high density areas in
> the towns in Tanganyika lags behind that in other territories
> I visited.[43]

The one major "success" of the Tanganyikan government's housing
program, according to the study, was that it involved very
limited public expenditure and planning machinery:

> [O]ur legislation permits the erection of traditional style
> housing in the towns, and in this respect it differs from
> elsewhere. This type of housing is particularly popular
> with Africans, especially in the coastal areas. It is
> designed for the accommodation of lodgers and there is no
> doubt that the existence of this type of housing has as-
> sisted towards relieving the housing problem in towns.
> Construction is usually in semi-permanent materials and the
> owners lease their plots on annual tenancies from Government
> where they are situated on public land. In recent years
> very marked improvements have become noticeable in the
> standard of construction of this type of housing, and today
> one finds some of these houses being erected on permanent
> foundations with more durable walls and galvanised iron
> roofs which although not so picturesque as "makuti" [thatched]
> are more weatherproof and fireproof. Some of these houses
> too are now being constructed totally in permanent materials
> and to improved designs prepared by the Government's African
> Housing Officer. This initiative is to be welcomed and
> every encouragement should be given to the owners to erect
> houses of this type to a standard which will enable them to
> secure long-term leases.[44]

To secure long-term rights, it should be noted, Africans
had to build in "permanent" materials as specified in the building codes; whatever the level of physical improvement, a traditional or "Swahili" house would never be considered permanent

---

[43]Ibid., p. 44.

[44]Ibid., p. 46. It should be noted that a similar system
obtained in Mombasa, which shared many of the same cultural
and physical characteristics as Dar es Salaam.

unless the materials of construction were completely changed.[45]
The report therefore recommended the relaxation of construction-
al standards following the Uganda pattern, but (at least through
the end of 1973) this still had not been done.

The major policy initiative taken by the colonial government following the Royal Commission report was the inauguration
of the African Urban House Loan Scheme in 1957. In six years
this revolving fund financed the private construction of 600
houses at low interest rates. The borrowers were those "who
could amass only a small down payment and whose relatively small
and unstable income made them poor risks."[46] Nevertheless,
institutional finance for private housing--even for those with
higher and more stable incomes--was very hard to obtain in pre-
Independence Tanganyika.

With the advent of Independence in 1961 until the Arusha
Declaration in 1967, Tanzania pursued two main strategies to
alleviate the pressure for housing and urban services by lower-
income groups: a building strategy and a land control strategy.[47]
The building strategy began with the formation of the National
Housing Corporation (NHC) in 1962. The corporation was given
a very broad mandate "for the provision of houses and other
buildings in Tanganyika by means of financial assistance and
otherwise."[48] After taking over from local authorities some
4,389 houses built under the African Urban Housing Scheme, the
corporation made "a heroic attempt to seriously cope with the
housing problem."[49] The first major program, concentrating in
Dar es Salaam at the initiative of President Julius Nyerere,
involved clearing some of the old "slums" on the periphery of

---

[45]For a critical view of this pattern in East Africa, see Saad
Yahya, "Permanence and Ephemera in Housing Development," East
Africa Journal, Vol. 6, No. 4 (April 1969), pp. 25-29.

[46]Manfred A. Bienefeld and Helmuth H. Binhammer, "Tanzania
Housing Finance and Housing Policy" in John Hutton, ed., Urban
Challenge in East Africa (Nairobi: East African Publishing
House, 1972), p. 181.

[47]A useful review of urban development policy in mainland
Tanzania is contained in Ministry of Lands, Housing and Urban
Development, Achievement in Ten Years of Independence (Dar es
Salaam, 1971).

[48]Laws of Tanzania, National Housing Corporation Act (Cap.
481).

[49]Bienefeld and Binhammer, p. 186.

the central business district (especially in Magomeni) and replacing them with new, single-storey houses which were rented out to the previous houseowners. During the first Plan period, from 1964 to 1969, about 70 percent of the 5,705 "low-cost" houses built by the NHC were part of the Dar es Salaam slum clearance scheme.[50] Although what constitutes a "low-cost" house has never been clearly defined either for or by the NHC, almost all its efforts have focused on this category of housing. Thus, during the first Plan period, the corporation received some £3.47 million from the Treasury in direct grants for low-cost housing. It was able to raise an additional £970,000 from the Federal Republic of Germany, which also gave technical aid (including the provision of a forceful General Manager). The total (£4.44 million) was only about 25 percent of the targeted figure in the Plan, however--most of the shortfall resulting from the NHC's failure to attract more overseas capital.

The second major approach to urban development through the 1960's was the control and allocation of land through the Lands Division--the land control strategy. Under a series of acts beginning in 1963,[51] all freehold land was converted to government leasehold, previous owners were obliged to pay rent to the government, and development conditions were laid down for the use of all urban land. (In practice, the development conditions for each leasehold plot were determined jointly by the Town Planning and Lands divisions.) The zoning policy of the colonial government--the division of residential urban land into low-, medium-, and high-density areas--was continued, but the emphasis in plot allocation and the provision of services was shifted from the low-density (i.e., former European) areas to the high-density (i.e., African) areas. In recent years, the Lands Division has prepared some 6,000 to 7,000 plots per year for allocation to the public, most of them in high-density areas. The bulk of the high-density plots are given out with year-to-year rights of occupancy. This allows the occupant, upon deposit of a down payment and a year's rent, to build a "temporary structure" using traditional materials. To obtain more permanent tenure (generally 33 years) in high-density areas, the occupant must pay a higher premium and rent and satisfy stiffer development conditions (as specified in the 1956 Building Code), involving significantly higher building expenses.

---

[50] For an evaluation of this scheme, see Gerhard Grohs, "Slum Clearance in Dar es Salaam" in Hutton, ed., Urban Challenge in East Africa, pp. 157-76.

[51] This legislation is discussed in detail in Ministry of Lands, Housing and Urban Development, Achievement . . ., pp. 14-17, and R.W. James, Land Tenure and Policy in Tanzania (Nairobi: East African Literature Bureau, 1971).

Before any new urban area is laid out for such development (usually following land-use recommendations of an urban "master" plan), the Tanzanian government pays full compensation to the people occupying the land. Thus, those who are living in an area scheduled for plot allocation or redevelopment--whether or not they have legal claims in terms of a strict application of land legislation--are fully compensated for the assessed value of their crops and buildings. Only after the occupants have been compensated can the area be developed. At this point the responsibility for the services that must be laid in (water, roads, sewerage systems or septic tanks, community facilities, etc.) is shared among a number of government divisions and parastatal organizations.

The Arusha Declaration of 1967, proclaiming the primacy of socialist rural development in Tanzania, significantly altered the direction of urban policy. First, the Declaration--published by the Tanganyika African National Union (TANU) National Executive Committee--argued that the burden of services and development in the urban areas was borne largely by the rural peasants. In addition, it proposed a leadership code which in effect separated the interests of higher party and government leaders from specifically urban-based enterprises.[52] With the publication of the Arusha Declaration, the Tanzanian government moved to nationalize some of the most important sectors of the urban industrial/commercial economy.

Soon after the Declaration was made public, the "Turner" report on wages, incomes, and prices policy was published by the government. Turner's analysis concluded that

> virtually the whole benefit of economic development since Independence has been allocated to employees, who are less than 10 per cent of the working population. . . . There is no doubt that the improvement in wage earners' standards has to a considerable extent occurred at the expense of the farmers who are the overwhelming majority of the population.[53]

The report argued further that, while this bias in favor of the urban sector was developing, inequities had also grown within

---

[52]For the text of the Arusha leadership code, see Julius Nyerere, Freedom and Socialism (Nairobi: Oxford University Press, 1968), p. 249.

[53]International Labour Office, Report to the Government of the United Republic of Tanzania on Wages, Incomes and Prices Policy (Government Paper No. 3, 1967; Dar es Salaam: Government Printer, 1967).

the body of wage-earners, favoring those working for the public services and the big firms. In accepting the substance of Turner's analysis, the government declared its intention to limit urban wage increases at the top end of the scale (the President had already cut the salaries of top civil servants and ministers), and to control prices for basic commodities.[54]

With the appearance of the Second Five-Year Plan, 1969-1974, a post-Arusha urban policy began to take shape. While the incomes and prices policies described above were incorporated into the Plan,[55] three new directions of development were indi-cated. First, moves were to be taken to decentralize certain government functions, and to locate new industries (wherever possible) away from Dar es Salaam. Eight towns around the country were selected for "concentrated urban development" over the Plan period.[56] Second, in order to maximize the spread of benefits to all classes of urban dwellers, the NHC was to increase its rate of house construction, while at the same time limiting itself to houses ranging in cost from £300 to £550 per unit.[57] Medium-cost houses would be financed either privately or through the newly created Permanent Housing Finance Corporation (PHFC), which lent at commercial rates of interest. Third, for the bottom end of the income scale, the NHC and the Ministry of Lands, Housing and Urban Development (formed in 1968 to unite most of the urban specialist divisions) were to develop a program for the provision of some 5,000 site and service plots per year. The plots were to be equipped with water, drainage, and founda-tions. The Plan projected that the public sector would provide from 35,000 to 40,000 houses and housing sites over the five-year period.

The next major urban policy initiative came in April 1971 with the government's announcement that it was taking over all rental buildings with a value of £5,000 and over.[58]

---

[54] Tanzania, Wages, Incomes, Rural Development, Investment and Price Policy (Government Paper No. 4, 1967; Dar es Salaam: Government Printer, 1967).

[55] Tanzania, Tanzania Second Five-Year Plan for Economic and Social Development: 1st July 1969-30th June, 1974, Vol. I (Dar es Salaam: Government Printer, 1969), pp. 205-207.

[56] These towns were Tanga, Arusha/Moshi, Mwanza, Mtwara, Mbeya, Morogoro, Dodoma, and Tabora. (See Tanzania, Tanzania Second Five-Year Plan . . ., p. 181.)

[57] Ibid., p. 191.

[58] The Acquisition of Buildings Act, 1971 applied to all

An Office of the Registrar of Buildings was created to administer the 2,900 buildings acquired, which had an estimated value of about £32.5 million.[59] The acquisitions were justified as a logical outcome of the country's socialism, but most of those who lost their houses and buildings were members of the Asian community. In any case, compensation was promised, landlords were permitted to continue to occupy the flats where they had been living, and tenants in acquired premises simply sent their monthly rent cheques to the Registrar of Buildings rather than to the landlord. The arrangements whereby the owners would be compensated were announced in 1973.[60]

But the problem of wealthy urban landlords was only the tip of the iceberg. Interministerial discussions had already begun in June 1970 concerning comprehensive housing policy and, in particular, the rents paid by lower-income groups. The Rent Restriction Act of 1962 had applied a fixed proportion of cost to all rents regardless of cost of construction, but the work of the Rent Tribunal had been confined mainly to Dar es Salaam and to landlord-tenant disputes over higher-cost dwellings.[61] Government housing and NHC-built housing where rents were collected by the corporation were exempted from the provisions of the act. In the post-Arusha atmosphere, some felt that government and parastatal officers, who were in most cases paying highly subsidized rents, should be required to pay in accordance with their incomes. The Cabinet decided in late 1972 to charge all government and parastatal employees occupying public housing according to their incomes. Those earning up to Shs. 750/- per month were to pay 7-1/2 percent of their gross monthly income in rent; those earning from Shs. 751/- to Shs. 1,500/- were to pay 10 percent; and those earning over Shs. 1,500/- were to pay 12-1/2 percent. Although an exact estimate of the impact of

---

buildings valued at Shs. 100,000/-, or renting for Shs. 833/- per month or more. Lists of the buildings and their owners were published in the newspapers. Because of mistakes, or successful applications to an appeals tribunal, about 300 of the original total acquired had been returned to their original owners by 1973.

[59]Ministry of Lands, Housing and Urban Development, Achievement . . . , p. 54.

[60]Daily News (Dar es Salaam), 14 February 1973.

[61]For details of how the tribunal worked in the 1960's, see Ripoti ya Mwaka 1967 ya Baraza la Kukariria Kodi za Nyumba [Annual Report, 1967 of the Rent Tribunal] (Dar es Salaam: Government Printer, 1969).

this decision was not made at the time, it was felt that the higher-income earners, who would be paying more rent under the new system, would in effect be subsidizing the lower-income earners, who would generally be paying lower rents than before. The net result would be less total income in rent for the government (thus a higher public subsidy to civil servants in general), but more equality in rentals between groups of public servants who had had the good fortune to obtain accommodation from their employers.

At the same time the rental changes were made, the government also decided: (1) to lower the loan ceiling on public-financed housing from £3,750 per house to £2,000 per house; (2) to selectively improve the services in existing squatter areas in towns and to upgrade squatter houses which met minimal standards; and (3) to revise existing building by-laws so as to permit maximum use of traditional and local building materials. A major institutional change was made: the Tanzania Housing Bank was set up on January 1, 1973, out of the old PHFC. Placed under the Treasury, the new Housing Bank would be able to borrow at less than commercial rates, which should substantially affect the financing of low-cost housing in urban areas and ujamaa villages.[62] In 1973 the Bank began working closely with the newly created Sites and Services Directorate in the Ministry of Lands, Housing and Urban Development to provide low interest "social loans" for a major national sites and services program.

The final, and most dramatic, urban policy decision during this period was President Nyerere's announcement on 1 November 1973 that the capital would be moved from Dar es Salaam to Dodoma, 300 miles to the west.[63] According to a resolution of the National Executive Committee of TANU, the move would take place gradually over ten years, at an estimated cost of £185.5 million. After a great deal of debate within the party over the question, only three of 18 Regions opposed the move. In announcing the party's decision the President emphasized "that the transfer of the capital would help stimulate development in the country because of the centrality of the new site."[64] While it is too early to evaluate the effects of this

---

[62]Details of the policy decisions outlined here can be found in Tanzania, Hali ya Uchumi wa Taifa Katika Mwaka 1972-73 [National Economic Survey 1972-73] (Dar es Salaam: Government Printer, 1973), pp. 85-86.

[63]Daily Nation (Nairobi), 2 October 1973.

[64]Ibid.

decision, it is clearly consistent with the overall scheme of decentralization of government functions which the government had begun in earnest over a year earlier.[65]

(2) Urban Policy Performance. The evolution of urban policy in independent Tanzania (especially in the period 1967-73) has been an expression of the need to achieve consistency with a dominant ideological current--i.e., movement toward a socialist society. The policy choices seem to have been rational and even laudable, but their implementation has often fallen far short of the original intent. To explain the deficiencies in implementation, some would point to insufficient ideological training and commitment among the leaders and middle-level bureaucratic cadres;[66] on a more general level, however, there has been a severe shortage of human and material resources--a shortage which has also beset other sectors of the development effort.[67] Whatever the reasons, the slow pace and occasionally misdirected bias of implementation has worked the greatest disadvantage on the urban poor.

Both the first and the second five-year Plans have given the NHC a major role in providing low-cost urban housing. During the first Plan period, however, the NHC was able to obtain only about 25 percent of the funds it had expected, and (as noted earlier) 70 percent of the low-cost housing it built in Dar es Salaam was part of a slum clearance scheme which added nothing to the existing housing supply. There were many problems involved in implementing this slum clearance scheme. For example, when the newly built houses were allocated by the NHC at a fixed rent of £4 to £5 per month to the former owners of "slum" houses in the area, the new tenants began subleasing most of the rooms in their houses, but were very lax in paying their own rents to the corporation. The reasons for their laxity in paying their rents were both economic and political. Economic: Before the slum

---

[65] On the reorganization of the central government in accordance with this scheme, see Julius Nyerere, Decentralization (Dar es Salaam: Government Printer, 1972).

[66] See, for example, Lionel Cliffe and Griffiths Cunningham, "Ideology, Organisation and the Settlement Experience in Tanzania" in L. Cliffe and John Saul, eds., Socialism in Tanzania, Vol. II (Nairobi: East African Publishing House, 1973), p. 139.

[67] For an argument along these lines applied to the trading and agricultural sectors, see G.K. Helleiner, "Socialism and Economic Development in Tanzania," Journal of Development Studies, Vol. 8, No. 2 (January 1972), pp. 183-204.

clearance project, most of the houseowners obtained the bulk of
their relatively meager incomes from renting out rooms. When
the new houses were built, they could charge little more for
rented rooms than before, but now they were saddled with substantial monthly payments to the NHC, which reduced their incomes
considerably. Political: The NHC could not evict the former
owners from their houses for nonpayment of rent because, as the
original inhabitants (wenyeji) of the area, many of them were
influential in TANU and could effectively resist the corporation's demands.

While the drafters of the second Plan stated that "the
absolute achievement of the National Housing Corporation had
been very considerable," they acknowledged that the net addition
to the housing stock of less than 400 units per year "just touched
the fringe of the housing problem."[68] When slum clearance was
halted in the late 1960's, the corporation found it difficult
to obtain funds. At present the NHC does some building for other
parastatals, and it has built for the middle-income marked through
loans from the PHFC (now the Tanzania Housing Bank), but the bulk
of its work is in low-cost housing, financed directly by Treasury
grants. These grants have diminished considerably in recent
years from a high of £1,070,000 in 1970/71 to £125,000 in 1973/74.
This diminution in funds reflects a number of factors: (1) the
Treasury's dissatisfaction over poor financial controls and rent
collection, (2) the NHC's failure to keep costs down (e.g., in
1973 the average low-cost house cost £920, though the second
Plan specified a ceiling of £550 per house), and (3) new development priorities which have reduced the funds available for urban
areas since the second Plan was adopted. With regard to (3),
specific mention should be made of the TANU Biennial Conference
in 1971, which emphasized the need to develop water, health, and
educational facilities in the rural areas. A target figure of
2,000 houses per year was set by the NHC, but it was able to
build only 138 low-cost units throughout the country in 1972/73--
about 7 percent of its original goal. Meanwhile, the corporation
had on record in 1972 over 18,000 "pending" applications for
low-cost houses for the whole country. From 1970-73, 5,500
applications for low-income housing were submitted to the Dar es
Salaam NHC office alone.[69]

In terms of numbers of plots produced, the surveyed plot
allocation program of the Lands Division has been much more successful than the NHC program. In 1971 the division issued 7,305

---

[68]Tanzania, Tanzania Second Five-Year Plan . . ., p. 189.

[69]Ministry of Lands, Housing and Urban Development, Sites and
Services Project (Dar es Salaam, 1973), p. 5.

new short-term rights of occupancy in urban areas; in 1972 the
figure was 6,331. But this was still far from enough to meet the
demand: for Dar es Salaam alone, the waiting list for high-
density plots was approximately 15,000 at the end of 1972. In
spite of direct Presidential pressure to speed up allocation,
the procedure remained cumbersome and expensive. A lot of money
had to be paid to compensate squatters and other interests before
land could be cleared for surveying, and when surveyed plots
were made available, services for the plots (such as roads,
water, schools) were rarely ready. The result was that there
was little controlled building, and squatters often moved back
on to the land. In a 1969 report the barriers created for the
poor and uneducated by land development procedures were described
as follows:

> The entire administrative process is designed to deal with
> the individual applicant who is prepared to undertake the
> development of an urban plot. Not only does this kind of
> system present problems for accommodating high rates of
> urban growth, but it is in fact quite inaccessible to the
> majority of the people. The legal framework and administra-
> tive process derive from a context quite foreign to most
> urban dwellers of Tanzania, particularly those who are
> relatively new to the urban environment. The aggressive,
> well educated and better paid urban dweller will be much
> more capable of getting a plot for himself than low-income,
> rural migrants who lack formal education and the skills
> relevant to urban living. Even if a person can successfully
> negotiate the administrative channels, know when and where
> to apply pressure, there is still the problem of raising
> the capital required to meet the development conditions of
> his right-of-occupancy. For the large number of households
> that must continually borrow to meet monthly living expenses,
> this is an insurmountable obstacle. Thus, while the present
> controls on land may help to maintain standards considered
> appropriate during the colonial era, they also effectively
> bar a majority of the population from legal access to land.[70]

A study done by the government in 1972 estimated that under nor-
mal conditions it could take 280 days for an applicant to receive
a right of occupancy to land scheduled for development.[71] In
view of the annual demand for new urban housing in the country

---

[70] A Proposal for an Urban Development Corporation in Tanzania
(prepared by PADCO, Inc., 1969), p. 20.

[71] Ministry of Lands, Housing and Urban Development, "Report
of Committee for Work Improvement," Schedule II (Dar es Salaam,
1972).

(estimated at 13,750 low-cost units in 1972),[72] it is clear that the combined efforts of the NHC and the plot allocation program were woefully inadequate.

A greatly expanded sites and services program was planned to complement the existing procedures. It will be recalled that the second five-year Plan called for 5,000 serviced sites per year. By the end of the Plan's third year, only 795 sites had been made available--all in a single area of Dar es Salaam. A recent evaluation succinctly describes the dilemma the government found itself in as a result of poor planning:

> An experimental project was initiated in 1970 at Kijitonyama in Dar es Salaam. Concrete slabs for 795 foundations were provided by NHC along with some 60 core houses. Average cost of slabs and core houses at Shs. 2,350/- plus high standards of infrastructure (approximately Shs. 7,000/- per plot) put the project beyond the reach of most low income families. The Government was therefore obliged to heavily subsidize the project in order that low income families could be settled on the plots and still repay loans for building materials.[73]

The problems of the Kijitonyama project did not dim the government's enthusiasm for the sites and services concept, but they underlined the necessity of careful financial planning. In 1973, following a study of the Ministry of Lands, Housing and Urban Development by a management consultant team, an Urban Development Department was set up within the ministry with its own Commissioner. Within the new department, a Sites and Services Directorate was given substantial authority to develop new schemes. In 1973 the directorate submitted a formal application to the World Bank for a massive five-year program involving 18,250 plots in Dar es Salaam, Mwanza, and Mbeya. A loan of Shs. 60 million was approved by the World Bank on July 2, 1974, and the program got underway shortly thereafter. An important part of this program was a recognition that squatting is both a necessary and a rational response to the accommodation problem: rents in squatter houses are lower than in conventional houses, and squatter areas are often conveniently located near places of work. The facilities in these areas are extremely poor, however, and the environment is often very unhealthy--especially during the

---

[72]Ministry of Lands, Housing and Urban Development, Urban Housing Needs 1972-1976 (Dar es Salaam: Ardhi Planning Unit, 1971).

[73]Ministry of Lands, Housing and Urban Development, Sites and Services Project, p. 9.

rainy seasons. Funds are therefore provided in the World Bank loan for the gradual improvement of some squatter areas through the building of roads and the installation of water and drainage systems.

The mere provision of services, however--even if they are free--does not always result in a more equitable distribution of urban benefits. Let us take urban water supplies as an example. For some years, the government's Water and Drainage Division has charged consumers for water only in houses where individual connections can be made (and meters attached). In squatter areas a presumably more benevolent practice has been followed: since extensive networks of pipes cannot be installed in "unplanned" neighborhoods, pipes are run in to one or two centrally located taps, where water is available to everyone free of charge. However, because squatter villages are often very large, and most women and working men cannot spend the time or make the effort necessary to carry individual pails of water back to their own houses, the work of supplying water consumers has become the specialized task of water carriers. These carriers, pushing carts which contain eight or ten four-gallon tins, sell the water to individuals. In 1972, the water carriers were charging--on the average--about 25 cents (Shs. -/25) per four-gallon tin. Families the author talked with purchased at least two tins per day, for a minimum monthly cost of Shs. 15/-, but in his government-owned house, he was charged at the rate of Shs. 6/- per thousand gallons--only 2.4 cents for four gallons. Thus squatters--in areas that are supplied with "free" water-- end up paying ten times more for equivalent amounts of water than do wealthier people living in surveyed, "legitimate" housing, where individual water connections with meters are installed. In addition, when there are water shortages, it always seems to be in the squatter areas that taps first run dry.

When the Acquisition of Buildings Bill was rushed through Parliament in April 1971, the Minister of Lands, Housing and Urban Development observed that the government had already nationalized big industries, banks, insurance companies, and wholesale and retail trade, but

> the opportunity still remains for exploiters to get high rents on large buildings in the cities. This strategy has strengthened the forces of privilege, especially in urban areas. This new revolutionary law [the Acquisition of Buildings Act], if passed by Parliament, will wipe away this opportunity and end privilege and exploitation.[74]

---

[74]Tanzania, Majadiliano ya Bunge [Hansard], 22 April-27 April 1971 (Dar es Salaam: Government Printer, 1971), col. 23. (The passage is translated by the author from the original Swahili.)

It was not merely a coincidence that most of the buildings affected by the new law were owned by Asians: the Asian community controlled the private commercial sector in Tanzania. The act was not manifestly racist, but the acquisitions resulted in many thousands of Asian families leaving the country. In addition, there was a great falloff in private building. Most private construction firms, which had invested their profits in buildings and used rents to provide working capital, were wiped out. No new housing resulted from the act, and it will be some time before the drop in construction capacity is redressed.

As noted earlier, a new income-based rental policy was announced by the government in early 1973, but it applied only to civil servants and parastatal employees living in government, parastatal, or NHC housing. Totally unaffected by the policy were almost all lower-income urban workers and the bulk of middle-income clerks and administrators, who had to find or build their own housing--often in squatter areas. The middle- and upper-income civil servants who came under the new regulations tended to feel that they were unfair: their incomes were not rising, but the new rents meant higher monthly payments for most.

The civil servants' attitudes toward the new rent scales must be seen in the light of the overall impact of the government's measures to redistribute urban incomes. Reginald Green summarizes the very real accomplishments of the redistribution efforts:

> Price changes have included an income policy which has narrowed the pre-tax range between the highest to the lowest paid public sector (including parastatal) worker from over 70-to-1 at Independence to about 18-to-1 today. Taking account of direct and indirect taxation, and the greater increases in prices affecting the higher-income groups, the effective differential in terms of consumption standards has fallen from about 60-to-1 to perhaps 13-to-1, including fringe benefits and access to public services.[75]

An important price has been paid for this policy, however. There has been a noticeable lowering of morale among the senior officials the government counts upon to carry out its socialist programs. Green argues that this loss of morale should not be exaggerated:

> Morale and incentives pose problems. . . . With the slower pace of citizen promotion, increasing numbers of senior

---

[75]Reginald H. Green, "Tanzania" in H. Chenery et al., Redistribution with Growth, p. 270.

citizen managers and civil servants face falling real incomes. Managerial and civil service salary scales in the
three neighboring countries and in the joint East African
services may be 50 percent to 200 percent higher, and
Tanzanians are acutely aware of this fact. As well, Tanzanians face the special strains of a more participatory
and decentralized system. However, morale is in fact
probably better than five years ago and at least as good
as in Kenya or Zambia.[76]

    One further aspect of Tanzanian urban policy can be con-
sidered here: the strategy of deconcentration outside of Dar es
Salaam. Of the approximately 30 major new industries set up in
the two years after the inception of the urban decentralization
plan, only ten were established outside Dar es Salaam; seven of
these ten were located in Arusha/Moshi. Thus only three of the
30 industries were shared by the seven least industrialized
growth towns.[77] Among the suggested explanations for the inef-
fectiveness of the industrial decentralization policy are that
no administrative machinery was set up to influence locational
decisions, and that many of the smaller designated towns did
not have a highly enough developed infrastructure to sustain
new industries. Another explanation offered is that the smaller
growth towns were not linked to the development of services in
the regions so as to provide support on a regional basis for
decentralized industrial growth.[78] The effects of the failure
to locate new industries outside Dar es Salaam are reflected in
several indices of growth. Thus in 1970 Dar es Salaam had 46.0
percent of the total recorded urban employment in Tanzania--up
from 44.2 percent the previous year.[79] In addition, for the
first two years of the second Plan the government was making
considerably higher urban investments in proportion to the total
than it had programmed in the Plan. (Estimates of the urban:
rural breakdown are given in Table 6.) The overall effect has
undoubtedly been to increase rural-urban migration to the largest
towns--in particular Dar es Salaam.

------

[76]Ibid., p. 273.

[77]Tanzania, The Economic Survey, 1970-71 (Dar es Salaam:
Government Printer, 1971), p. 103.

[78]A.C. Mascarenhas and C.-F. Claeson, "Factors Influencing
Tanzania's Urban Policy," African Urban Notes, Vol. 6, No. 3
(Fall 1972), p. 33.

[79]Tanzania, Survey of Employment and Earnings 1970 (Dar es
Salaam: Bureau of Statistics, 1972), p. 37.

Table 6

PROPORTIONS OF TOTAL CENTRAL GOVERNMENT DEVELOPMENT
EXPENDITURE IN URBAN AND RURAL AREAS DURING SECOND
FIVE-YEAR PLAN: 1969-1974

Area of Expenditure	1969-74: Whole Plan Period	Proportions of Expenditure			
		1969/70		1970/71	
		Budgeted	Actual	Budgeted	Estimated Actual
Rural areas	56.0%	48.8%	46.8%	48.3%	48.5%
Urban areas	33.9	39.6	41.1	40.3	44.3
National infra-structure	10.1	11.6	12.1	11.4	9.2
Totals	100.0	100.0	100.0	100.0	100.0

Source: Tanzania Sites and Services Project (Dar es Salaam: Ministry of Lands, Housing and Urban Development, 1973), p. 3.

The program for decentralization of administrative functions has been more successful than that for industry. Under the new Regional Development Directors appointed in 1972, significant town planning, surveying and land allocation functions are now undertaken in the Regions. There are critical shortages of staff at the regional level, but the situation is improving, and for the financial year 1973/74, annual budgets were drawn up by the Regions themselves in cooperation with the Prime Minister's Office. The decision to move the capital to Dodoma will certainly give impetus to the decentralization effort, even though it is likely to take many years to complete the move.

Chapter III

THE GROWTH OF SQUATTING IN DAR ES SALAAM

The analysis in the preceding chapter has shown that the urban policies implemented during the post-Independence period in Tanzania have not kept pace with the rapid urbanization and the accompanying growing demands for services and accommodation. Not only has the gross output of new low-cost accommodation been insufficient, but the impact of government policy has been predominantly to the advantage of the upper- and middle-income groups in the urban population. These shortfalls in policy implementation and biases in policy impact have provided the context for a dramatic increase in urban squatting--particularly in Dar es Salaam. In this chapter we shall discuss the growth of squatting in Dar es Salaam, and some of the important legal/administrative and economic factors that have contributed directly to it.

A. Squatters Defined

As referred to in this paper, "squatters" are people who unlawfully occupy urban land. Lawful occupation of urban land in Tanzania requires a Right of Occupany issued by the Lands Division; this document must be based on a formal plot survey. Thus the definition of "squatters" implies that squatter houses are built either on (1) unsurveyed urban land or (2) surveyed land without formal right of occupancy. Squatters who live on surveyed land in the towns rarely build their homes with any reference to surveyed plot boundaries. The definition of squatting used here is both heuristic (it makes possible the designation and enumeration of squatter houses from aerial photographs) and in accordance with local usage (the Swahili expression for squatters is watu wanaojenga ovyo ovyo--lit., "people who build in a random fashion"). Accordingly, a "squatter area" is an area in which the people have built their houses without regard to survey boundaries, whether or not such boundaries have been established. In the following discussion, all those living in squatter areas will be considered squatters, including both houseowners and their tenants.[1]

---

[1]Recent correspondence (April 1975) indicates that although the term squatter is now being used less and less in official circles, no alternative term has replaced it.

The definition used here is admittedly a narrowly legal one, but bears a direct relation to important differences in urban living standards. In general, the courts in Tanzania have been unwilling to prosecute squatters merely because their occupation of urban land is not in accordance with a strict interpretation of the law. Squatter houses may be as good as (if not better than) many houses built on surveyed plots to which the houseowners have legal rights of occupancy. However, most of the squatter areas have much poorer access to urban amenities than do comparable high-density areas where houses are built on surveyed plots. Roads, schools, water and electric facilities, refuse disposal services, surface water drainage, and septic tank emptying services in squatter areas are markedly inferior to those in non-squatter areas.

B. The Historical Pattern

There is little evidence that squatting (or the growth of "shanties") in Dar es Salaam became a problem for the Tanganyikan government until the late 1950's. One reason for this is reflected in the 1931-1967 population figures for the city (see Table 7). From 1931 to 1943 the African population of Dar es Salaam grew at an average rate of only 2.8 percent per year. Then from 1943 to 1948 the yearly average growth of the African population in the capital rose significantly to 9.0 percent. The census figures do not indicate the year-to-year fluctuations, but the average rate of growth of the African population reached a high of 11.1 percent per year from 1948 to 1952. Following Independence, the rate of growth slowed down somewhat, but with an increase in wage employment associated with the development of Dar es Salaam, the growth rate of the African component of the city's population rose again to an average of at least 9.0 percent per year from 1957 to 1967.

A second reason why squatting was not a problem is that, given relatively modest numbers of urban migrants, the Tanganyikan government was able to provide enough new plots and--through its building program--new houses in the high-density areas to keep up with the demand. The plots were made available in large part from public land, for which short-term (i.e., year-to-year) rights of occupancy were issued. These occupancy rights carried no building covenant (i.e., an obligation to erect buildings of a minimum specified value), which meant that houseowners could build as they wished in traditional materials, and the cost of services (roads, water, drainage) was substantially subsidized by the government. As long as such plots were available, there was little economic incentive for would-be houseowners to build on unsurveyed plots with nonexistent services. Even where long-term rights of occupancy (generally for 33 years) were granted in high-density areas, lessees were obliged only to erect

Table 7

POPULATION GROWTH IN DAR ES SALAAM: 1931-1967

Year	African Population	Total Population	African Population Growth Rate from Previous Period
1931	24,000	34,300	
1943	33,000	45,100	2.8%
1948	50,765	69,277	9.0
1952	77,330	99,140	11.1
1957	93,363	128,742	3.8
1967	221,328[a]	272,821	9.0[a]

[a]This is an underestimate, since only those respondents who reported their racial origin were counted in the tabulation. Assuming there was an equal proportion of underestimation for all racial groups, the African population in 1967 would have been 235,197, and the 1957-67 African growth rate 9.7 percent per annum.

Sources: J.E.G. Sutton, Dar es Salaam: City, Port and Region (Dar es Salaam: Tanganyika Notes and Records, No. 71, 1970), p. 19; Tanzania, Statistical Abstract 1970 (Dar es Salaam, 1972), pp. 46, 52.

buildings of a value of at least Shs. 15,000/- per plot. In addition, plots were always available on private freehold land before Independence.

A third reason for the lack of concern about squatting is that, until the latter part of the colonial period, squatters could be evicted from public or private land which was "ripe for development" with little or no ex gratia payment of compensation. It was not until the late 1950's that the government, to placate nationalist critics, began to give generous compensation to squatters who had to be removed from newly planned areas. (Once this policy was instituted, it was extremely difficult for an independent African government to discontinue it.) This encouraged squatting. At the same time, the colonial (and later the independent) government was becoming increasingly reluctant to use force to evict squatters from prime urban land.

A fourth reason why squatting was not a problem is that the way in which the larger towns (and especially Dar es Salaam) grew during the colonial period tended to limit the growth of squatter areas. Large areas of the cities were planned, and in the semi-rural "villages" on the outskirts which were inevitably swallowed up by the extension outward of urban boundaries, the land was generally held under traditional law. Settlement around these village nuclei was encouraged by the growth of Dar es Salaam; however, little attention seems to have been paid to the planning or servicing of these areas. In A Survey of Dar es Salaam, written in 1957, J.A.K. Leslie distinguishes between rural settlements on the outskirts of the town, where each house had an adjacent subsistence plot, and what he terms "villages." In a description worth quoting at length, he states that the term Village

> is intended to cover both original villages which have become engulfed by the advancing town . . . and clusters of houses which have sprung up within the town as a result of urban conditions. The latter class includes parts of Kipawa and Mtoni where a rural scatter of huts has as population pressure increased become a Village, squeezing out the subsistence plots; and places such as Toroli in Keko which sprang up purely as shanties at a time of great and sudden shortage of housing, but have since begun to evolve with improved houses into Villages within the town.
> Where a Village is an engulfed original village, its case is very similar to that of the Rural areas, where the originally fairly homogeneous population . . . has been supplemented by accretions both before and after being engulfed. This original population remains the "owners" (wenyeji) of the Village, and the others as they come and settle are expected to fit themselves into things as they find them; to accept the original spokesmen as their own,

and to fit themselves into the order of esteem which has
grown up through generations.

On the other hand, when a Village has arisen as a shanty
town one would suppose that these considerations would not
apply; for the shanties sprang up so quickly, in the immediate post-war period, that it seemed like a rush of new
immigrants similar to those who flow in, in a single month,
when a new town-planned suburb is demarcated and opened up.
In fact, however, there is a vital difference: in a town-
planned suburb, such as Temeke, the land acquired by Government is empty one day, and the next day--so to speak--par-
celled out to a large number of newcomers, none of whom
receives his rights to the land much before the others; they
all move in together as Government's tenants, in a single
undifferentiated block, with no leaders or led, no traditional elders, in fact no framework of society into which a newcomer can fit himself in his appropriate place. In no case
did the building of the shanty towns happen in this way; . . .
although the original villagers were to a large extent flooded
out by the large number of newcomers, many of whom squat
without any permission from an earlier squatter . . . there
remain still some recognized leaders and led. These shanties
are an extreme case: intermediate are the old villages which
although they did not pre-date Dar es Salaam, date back for
a long way and were originally settlements, not part of a
continuous block of urban housing but satellites of what is
now the central town. . . .[2]

Unless a "village" was freehold land (the case with Buguruni)
when it was incorporated within township boundaries, the rights
of the original occupants were recognized, and they could only
be removed after payment of compensation. Thus if the government
wanted to develop an area newly incorporated within a township
boundary where traditional housing had been built before the
extension of the boundary, it would first have to compensate the
occupants of the land. Most of the larger towns had squatters
of this type, but they were not considered a problem because the
land they occupied was not required for alternative development.
The process of accretion and unplanned growth (described above
by Leslie for Dar es Salaam in the 1940's and 1950's) did not
produce confrontation between planners and "villagers" as long
as enough unoccupied land existed for new residential and industrial areas.

In the late 1950's the time when there was adequate
available land for planning purposes seems to have come to an
end. The central government began to pay particular attention

---

[2]Leslie, pp. 97-98.

to "the problem of squatters," especially in Dar es Salaam. In 1959, as a result of a dispute over subsidies between the central government and the City Council of Dar es Salaam, the council refused to give planning consent for short-term rights of occupancy in high-density areas. Africans who had built Swahili houses on surveyed plots were served with demolition notices by the council. By the time this dispute was resolved, many squatters had already begun to build on unsurveyed land, since there no longer seemed to be any advantage in building on surveyed plots. One section where large-scale squatting took place at this time was in an area called Chang'ombe kwa Nuba, which had been planned and pre-serviced for industrial plots. By early 1961 some 100 houses stood on the site, with 25 or 30 more in the course of construction. This matter was brought to the attention of the Council of Ministers (i.e., the Cabinet), which decided that the squatters should be compensated, but that compulsion should be used to evict them only as a last resort. Subsequently, while negotiations were going on between the government and the squatters, the Minister for Lands, Forests and Wildlife issued a public notice to the effect that the government would not pay compensation for buildings erected after the date of the notice. However, by the time the matter was brought before the Cabinet again in March 1962 (Tanganyika having in the meantime become independent), a total of 211 houses had been built on the Chang'ombe site. At this meeting, the Cabinet took a slightly different position: eviction notices were to be issued to the squatters, but they would be paid full compensation and given help in moving building materials to surveyed plots in other areas. At the end of 1963 the squatters were still there, however, having refused the plots offered to them in surveyed high-density areas. Meanwhile, other organized "invasions" of squatters had taken place: Buguruni, the old Aerodrome area, and the Hannah Nassif estate in Kinondoni had all experienced a large influx. Despite the political intention to remove and control the squatters, force was rarely used against them, and their numbers continued to grow.

The proliferation of squatters in Dar es Salaam at this time suggests that the approach of Independence played a major role. As the Sunday News observed in October 1962, there was a massive rural-urban move to the larger towns in anticipation of the benefits of uhuru:

Since last December many thousands of rural Tanganyikans have moved into towns. Dar es Salaam has had its share; so too have the other urban areas. The migrants came in search of a monthly wage, of bright lights, of a better standard of living than the subsistence level they knew in their villages and shambas.
Some of them found a monthly wage but many more have not and, faced with the task of housing their families, they moved

into vacant residential and industrial plots and there built
for themselves makuti-roofed houses.

These squatters pose several problems. They constitute
a danger to public health; they impede development. . . .

Strong arm methods--such as the use of the police--to
remove them will not provide a lasting solution. . . .

First, a decision must be taken on where to resettle
these people--whether to keep them in Dar es Salaam or
rehabilitate them up-country. Sending them back to their
shambas may prove a waste of time and effort; perhaps the
wisest course would be to resettle them on properly surveyed
plots with sanitation facilities and a pure water supply. . . .

We doubt whether the City Council or other local councils
have resources for such operations in the towns of this
country without assistance from the Government. But the
job must be done--quickly and properly.

We do not want the urban areas in Tanganyika to be ringed
with shanty towns, with all the filth and squalor that is
invariably associated with them.[3]

The newspaper's expression of caution about the use of force
against low-income Africans, while sensible and humane, was also
politically expedient: the new national government, strongly
committed to social justice for its people, would use compulsion
only as an absolutely last resort.

Whatever the reasons, the squatter population showed a
steady increase. Though government agency figures are not always
reliable and are often based on different counting procedures at
different times, they are cited here because they give an indication of the official estimate of the squatter problem. In 1960,
the Land Office Agent estimated that there were 5,000 squatter
houses in Dar es Salaam. In 1963, a comprehensive survey by the
Town Planning Division, based on aerial photographs taken in
February 1962, showed a total of 7,000 squatter houses. Of
these, 2,330 were in "traditional villages within the planned
city," 3,560 were in "squatter areas" proper, 400 were in "traditional villages outside present development areas," and 710 were
in "scattered rural occupation."[4] The Town Planning Division
estimated the total to have risen to 9,000 houses in 1965.

The next major count of squatter houses in Dar es Salaam
was carried out by the Planning Unit of the Ministry of Lands,

---

[3] Sunday News (Dar es Salaam), 14 October 1962.

[4] "Traditional Villages and Squatting in the City of Dar es
Salaam: The Extent of the Problem and Cost of Solution" (Memo
by Commissioner for Town Planning, 1963; Dar es Salaam: Ministry
of Local Government).

Housing and Urban Development, using 1969 aerial photographs.
This count showed a total of 14,720 houses in fourteen main
areas of the city.[5] The most recent count, again by the Ministry
Planning Unit, carefully updated the figures using aerial photographs taken in September 1972. The 1972 count showed 27,981
squatter houses in the greater Dar es Salaam planning area--an
average compound yearly increase from 1969-72 of 24 percent.
Over the 1963-72 period, the average compound yearly increase
was 16.6 percent. (Figures for the major areas in 1972 are
shown in Table 8.) At the same time the 1972 count was being
made from aerial photographs, the Ministry Planning Unit took
part in a sample survey study of some 500 squatter houses selected
at random throughout the city. This study showed that, while
the number of occupants per house varied considerably according
to house size and distance from the city center, the average
occupancy rate was eight persons per house. Applying this occupancy rate to the largest squatter area in Dar es Salaam--
Manzese--produces a population of at least 54,952 (the occupancy
rate for Manzese is probably higher than average). This is
larger than the projected population in 1972 of Mwanza--Tanzania's
third largest town!

The results of another study corroborated the 1969-72
growth figures produced by the ministry. Assuming an annual
growth rate of 24 percent, the number of squatter houses built
in 1972 would have been 5,348. The National Housing and Building
Research Unit calculated that an estimated 1.16 million mangrove
poles brought to Dar es Salaam in 1972 would have been sufficient
to build 6,000 traditional-style (Swahili) houses.[6] The difference between 5,348 and 6,000 can easily be accounted for by
variations in the sizes of the houses constructed and by the
fact that mangrove poles are also used for house maintenance
and construction of mabanda (ancillary sheds).

The great increase in the squatter population in Dar es
Salaam must have been a major factor in the overall population
growth of the city. In the absence of census figures since
1967, we can begin with the 1967 population of 273,000 for the
portion of Dar es Salaam within city council boundaries, with a
15 percent addition for the built-up portion outside the boundaries. This gives a figure of 313,950 for greater Dar es Salaam

---

[5]John Leaning, "Squatter Housing in Dar es Salaam" (Dar es
Salaam: Ministry of Lands, Housing and Urban Development, 1972).

[6]O. Therkildsen and P. Moriarty, Economic Comparison of Building
Materials: Survey of Dar es Salaam (Dar es Salaam: National
Housing and Building Research Unit, Ministry of Lands, Housing
and Urban Development, 1973), p. 13.

THE GROWTH OF SQUATTING IN DAR ES SALAAM

Table 8

SQUATTER HOUSES IN DAR ES SALAAM BY AREA:
1972

Area	Number of Houses
Buguruni	3,020
Chang'ombe	1,345
Ilala	570
Kawe	714
Keko/Gerezani	2,240
Kigogo	1,643
Kinondoni/Mwanayamala	1,572
Kipawa	1,242
Kisutu	116
Kurasini	363
Manzese	6,869
Mbezi	175
Msasani	624
Mtoni	3,855
Tandika	2,426
Temeke	214
Ubungo	675
Vingunguti	130
Total	27,981

Source: Ministry of Lands, Housing and Urban
Development survey.

in 1967. Applying the average intercensal growth rate from 1957 to 1967 of 7.7 percent to this figure, we obtain an estimated population for Dar es Salaam of 364,160 in 1969. If eight persons per house in the squatter areas is assumed, the squatter population in 1969 would have been 117,760, leaving 250,240 in the regular housing areas of the city. From 1969 on, we know the growth rate of the squatter areas, but not the growth rate in the regular housing areas. If we assume a natural population increase of 1.8 percent per year (the estimated average natural increase in the urban areas of Tanzania)[7] and take into account the fact that not much building took place in the planned areas of Dar es Salaam during this period, an estimated growth rate of 4 percent per annum for the planned parts of the city does not seem unreasonable. On the basis of these calculations, there would have been some 224,000 people in the squatter areas and 281,000 people in the planned areas of the city in 1972--a total of 505,000. This suggests that in 1972 approximately 44 percent of the total population of greater Dar es Salaam lived in squatter areas. On the basis of the same calculations, the growth of the total population in 1972 over the previous year would have been 12 percent. The rate of growth of the whole population should have risen as the squatter population percentage increased, since the squatter component had been growing much more rapidly than the population in the regular housing areas. Thus, as a result of the rapid growth in its squatter areas, the rate of growth of Dar es Salaam has become much higher than the 7.7 percent per annum growth recorded between 1957 and 1967.

The "Causes" of Squatting

Just as the "problems" of squatter areas cannot be analyzed in isolation from the social structure and political economy of the entire society, the "causes" of squatting cannot be reduced to narrowly technical factors. In this paper it has been suggested that the colonial educational system, biases in urban policies which discriminated against low-income groups, and political constraints on the post-Independence government which circumscribed the use of force at a time when there was an unusually large urban influx have all contributed importantly to the growth of squatting. In the following section we will concentrate on some of the more immediate structural factors which acted as pre-conditions for the rapid rate of increase in squatting in recent years. These are classified into two main categories: legal/administrative and economic.

---

[7]Claeson and Egero, *Migration and the Urban Population*, p. 20.

A. Legal/Administrative Factors

As noted earlier, many traditional houses were built under traditional (customary) rights of occupancy on unsurveyed land surrounding the urban areas. Where this land remains outside township boundaries, occupation of the land without legal title is not, strictly speaking, illegal--unless the Region has been declared a compulsory registration area. The Coast Region (which includes Dar es Salaam) was so declared in January 1971, the notice expiring on June 30, 1971. After the latter date, all occupied land in the whole Region without formal, legal title (Right of Occupancy) from the Lands Division was technically in breach of the law.

Within townships, however, or in areas where township boundaries have expanded to embrace land held under traditional tenure, all land must be registered according to the Freehold Titles (Conversion) and Government Leases Act of 1963.[8] Since all land is now vested in the state, every user of land (including a houseowner) must have a Right of Occupancy issued by the Commissioner for Lands. A second legal requirement arises under the Town and Country Planning Ordinance according to which all buildings in declared "planning areas" (i.e., in all the large towns in Tanzania) must receive planning "consent" from the local authority according to terms specified in the Townships Ordinance. Only those with legal titles to their land can apply for planning consent. If land is developed without planning consent, the local authority has power under Section 72 of the Town and Country Planning Ordinance to order demolition. If the demolition order is not complied with, the local council can enter upon the land, demolish any unauthorized structures, and recover expenses.

Curiously, the law giving local authorities powers to demolish directs the penalties toward the "owner" of the land. Since all land is vested in the state, the government becomes responsible in the first instance for all illegal use of its own land. The government has powers under the Land Ordinance to evict any person unlawfully using and occupying land, but offenders are subject to fines only. A Lands Division report argues that the procedure prescribed under the law for evicting squatters is too slow to be effective:

A person unlawfully using and occupying public land may be "evicted" at the instance of the Land Office. The proceedings are civil and not criminal in nature. A notice is

---

[8]The most comprehensive treatment of land law pertaining to urban areas of mainland Tanzania can be found in R.W. James, Land Tenure and Policy in Tanzania, pp. 93-166.

first served upon the illegal occupier by a Land Office Official (or Internal Revenue Officer) requiring him to quit on or before a stated date.

If the notice is ignored the Officer concerned then files a plaint in the Resident Magistrate's Court where the land is situated asking for (a) a declaration that the defendant is in unlawful occupation of land and (b) an order for the defendant to surrender the land to the Government "within such a period and upon such term . . . as to the court shall seem just." Section 23 (1), Land Ordinance, Cap. 113.

A squatter who remains in occupation after the date when he was ordered to surrender the land, or who returns to the land, is guilty of an offence and liable to a fine not exceeding two thousand shillings, and in the case of a continuing offence, an additional fine not exceeding five hundred shillings for every day during which he continues to occupy the land: Section 23 (2), Land Ordinance. There is no provision for imprisonment or for the manner in which the physical eviction of the offender may be carried out, or as to what would happen if a squatter refused to pay the fine.

This procedure is slow, cumbersome and, to a Government anxious and impatient about land development, ineffective and not very helpful. It is necessary to have a quick and effective procedure for putting land under occupation in Government's hands, when need be, for industrial or other purposes. Section 23 of the Land Ordinance, Cap. 113 should be amended accordingly.[9]

As things stand now, the law permits demolition of illegal buildings by local authorities provided there is agreement by the Ministry of Lands, Housing and Urban Development. If squatters refuse to permit their houses to be demolished, or if they refuse entry onto the land they occupy, the government must be prepared to use force if the law is to be effective. Unlike neighboring Kenya, however, in Tanzania the government has on the whole not been prepared to use force against squatters. As a result, the demolition law has become virtually inoperative.

The following example illustrates the practical difficulties of enforcing the laws against urban squatters: In early 1963 the city council of Dar es Salaam decided to press for the eviction of a large number of squatters within the city. Notices were served upon the occupants of the squatter houses; when these were ignored, the council forwarded the names and location of the offenders to a magistrate's court in Dar es Salaam. The

---

[9]Lands Division, "The Problem of Squatters in Urban Areas" (unpublished memorandum, March 1967), p. 17.

number involved was over 1,000, and the Regional Local Courts Officer asked the Regional Commissioner for guidance because "unless arrangements are made to re-house the occupants, the Local Courts might precipitate a dangerous situation." The Regional Commissioner agreed that firm action against the squatters should be taken immediately, but he hesitated to support the council unless the court was "very strongly backed up by Central Government, if necessary with the Field Force." Said the Commissioner:

> It is clear that the action intended by the Council is a desperate measure brought about through years of neglect. Had the Council's inspectors taken action at the early stages of these settlements, the public could have been prevented from building without undue disturbance or difficulty.

In the end, the council's orders were not dealt with by the courts.

Similar cases, in which the council was prepared to evict but needed support from the courts, which in turn needed but could not obtain unequivocal political and police backing, have occurred on various occasions in subsequent years. The only successful mass relocation involved squatters living on the former Hannah Nassif estate in Kinondoni. The relocation was successful because the Hannah Nassif squatters were allocated a large block of surveyed plots in Mwananyamala, very close to their original location. In addition, these squatters were given surveyed plots (at regular fees) in preference over other waiting-list applicants, after having been fully compensated by the government for the removal of their houses! Such a combination of nearby free land and preferential treatment for a large number of squatters was not to be duplicated.

The difficulty of obtaining surveyed plots has been a factor of crucial importance in the increase in squatting. Before Independence, a relatively modest demand for high-density, low-cost plots in the towns was adequately met through the issuance by the government of short-term, renewable rights of occupancy, or through the leasing of their land by private landowners for a yearly rent. After Independence, with the termination of freehold rights to land, the burden of satisfying a much greater demand for such plots fell entirely on the government. In most centers, the issuing of rights of occupancy (now carried out by Regional officials) has been inadequate to meet the demand for plots. This probably has less to do with procedural complications in the Lands Division, which finally issues the occupancy rights, than with the related problems of getting funds from the Treasury for compensation, and coordinating the actions of the Valuation Division (for valuation of existing structures and plot

premia), the Town Planning Division (for plot layouts), and the
Surveys and Mapping Division (for plot surveys). Whatever the
reasons for the delays, in Dar es Salaam there was a large back-
log of applications for high-density plots in 1973.

Confronted with backlogs, individuals who need housing
quickly will obtain plots in an informal way--even if the trans-
actions cannot be registered with legal title. This can be seen
as a continuation of the traditional system of obtaining land,
where a newcomer made a payment to the mzee (elder) in charge
of allocating land on behalf of a clan or local group. In 1973,
informal payments for building plots in Dar es Salaam ranged
upwards from Shs. 150/- depending on the area, even though the
transaction conveyed no legal rights to the land. Despite the
fact that legal, short-term rights of occupancy cost only Shs.
30/- to Shs. 40/- per year, most would-be houseowners prefer to
pay a lot of money for a plot in a squatter area of their
choice rather than to wait their turn for a legally allocated
government plot at a low rental. As a recent study shows, such
behavior is quite reasonable:

> Although provision of surveyed plots has increased on a
> national scale from about 4,740 in 1969 to around 6,700
> in 1972, procedural delays and lack of compensation funds
> have limited the amount of high density plots available
> to low income urban families. Moreover, when plots are
> ultimately prepared, they are most often allocated to
> displaced squatters, thereby resulting in little or no
> reduction in the waiting list for plots. For example,
> out of 1,454 high density plots prepared in Tabata East,
> outside of DSM, in 1971, 1,370 were allocated to former
> squatters in the area who had prior claims. Of the 84
> remaining plots which were offered to applicants on the
> District Land Officer's waiting list, 72 were refused due
> primarily to the absence of any urban services in the area.
> The lack of services and access to surveyed urban plots has
> also led to the situation where most families who have been
> allocated these plots have not chosen to build upon them.[10]

Although squatters who obtain land informally have no
legal documents to support their claims, they appear to feel that
they have some clearly defined rights. One is their right to
use the land, which is clearly recognized by everyone living in
their neighborhood. Another is their right of ownership of
houses and crops, which the government explicitly recognizes
through its payment of compensation (based on elaborate fee
schedules) when an eviction takes place. Some squatters in Dar

---

[10]Tanzania, Sites and Services Project, p. 9.

66

es Salaam attempt to establish rights by paying the Urban House Tax[11] to the local authority. In some squatter areas (e.g., Buguruni), almost every houseowner pays this tax annually. Although the squatters may feel that payment of this tax (with the receipt provided) should give them rights of occupancy, the government takes the position that the house tax is merely a charge for services rendered. (In squatter areas where the house tax is paid, the city council--at least before its abolition at the end of 1973--was providing for the maintenance of roads, refuse collection, and an ambulance and fire brigade service.)

An attempt to control squatting in Dar es Salaam administratively was initiated in March 1969 with the establishment of a cadre of "land rangers" under the Legal Section of the Lands Division. Some 12 rangers, selected mainly from among TANU Youth League members, were based at Ilala administrative headquarters under the charge of a squatter control officer. The officer, a popular former city councillor, was a Zaramo (the largest local ethnic group) with deep roots in the area. The land rangers have succeeded in curtailing the building of some new houses by reminding owner-builders that their actions are illegal and by harassing the mafundi (artisans), but their presence seems to have had little effect on the rate of squatter growth.

The effectiveness of the land rangers has been limited by at least four factors. First, squatters often resort to evasive practices--such as building by night--or threats of violence when harassed by the rangers. Second, the rangers feel that they have only moral authority to evict squatters--i.e., that the Land Ordinance does not give them the legal power to evict illegal builders from government land. Third, some TANU leaders at the local level appear to be involved in the selling of plots to prospective squatters, which would not be surprising, since TANU local leaders are often elders and would simply be continuing a practice that began well before the mid-1960's. Moreover, TANU local leaders say that they cannot help enforce the laws against squatting because if they did so they would not be reelected. This suggests that TANU's problems in enforcing local regulations in the urban areas are not dissimilar from what has been shown in studies of rural Tanzania--most notably a study by Jean O'Barr of the Pare ward of Mbaga[12] and by J.S.

---

[11]This tax, which was raised from Shs. 75/- to Shs. 100/- per house in 1973, was a major source of revenue for the city council, bringing in some Shs. 1 million per year.

[12]Jean F. O'Barr, "Cell Leaders in Tanzania," African Studies Review, Vol. 15, No. 3 (December 1972), pp. 437-65.

Quorro of three villages in the Mbulu district.[13] Since TANU
is well-organized at the local level in most of the squatter
areas in Dar es Salaam, TANU leaders have served effectively in
preventing Draconian action against squatting. The fourth problem
faced by the land rangers in their efforts to control squatting
is that they cannot offer squatters alternative surveyed plots
on which to build, except in limited cases where whole areas
have been surveyed for the occupants of a specified redevelopment
zone. When, on any given day, several hundred squatter houses
are in the course of construction all around the city, the alternative sites which can be offered by the rangers are limited
by the inaccessibility of the areas opened for legal plot alloca-
tions. If a great number of surveyed plots could be made available quickly in accessible areas, the efforts of the land rangers
would be aided considerably.

B. Economic Factors

        Whatever the legal/administrative factors may be which
help to explain why squatting is inevitable in Dar es Salaam,
the massive scale of squatting can only be explained by its
economic profitability. The discussion to follow will deal with
two aspects of the economics of squatting: (1) cost of construction and returns on investment and (2) the system of cash compensation.

        Cost of Construction and Returns on Investment. Almost
all squatter houses built in Dar es Salaam are some variation
of the "Swahili house." This is the most common urban house type
along the East African coast. Among the distinctive features of
its design are its overall rectangular shape, a covered verandah
at the front, independent rooms leading off a main central cor-
ridor, a courtyard (sometimes enclosed) to the rear, and utility
rooms (usually including a storage room, toilet, and cooking
room) adjoining the courtyard in the back. Until recently,
Swahili houses were built almost entirely of local, traditional
materials. The most important of these materials were boriti
(mangrove poles used for the internal framework of the roof and
walls), udongo (clay or mud daubed on the sides to form walls),
and makuti (palm-leaf thatch sewn together in strips to form the
roof cover). Most people now prefer to use more permanent
materials in construction, especially since this reduces the
need for maintenance work. Improvements in building materials
and procedures include the substitution of corrugated iron roofing

----

[13]"The Modern Local Leadership and the Problem of Effectiveness" (unpublished dissertation; University College, Dar es
Salaam, March 1969).

sheets (mabati) for thatch, the addition of coral chips or blocks to the walls, the substitution of cement blocks for earthwork, the plastering and painting of wall surfaces, and the construction of a cement-covered, raised plinth for the floor.

The Swahili house has become popular along the East African coast for a number of reasons. First, the design of the house satisfies important practical and security needs. The courtyard can be used for laundry and cooking, and can be enclosed by a wall on either side to safeguard the privacy of Muslim women or of lodgers in polyglot, often transient neighborhoods. A feature of the Swahili house which makes it popular among landlords is that most of the individual rooms are spatially independent of both the courtyard (and its communal or family activities) and of each other. This facilitates the renting of rooms to lodgers without undue inconvenience to the rest of the household.

A second important reason for the popularity of the Swahili house is its relatively low cost of construction. A study of the cost of an "improved" Swahili-style house in Dar es Salaam showed that in 1971 the owner would have to pay Shs. 6,350/- to have a four-room house built.[14] Assuming that all the rooms were rented at Shs. 30/- per month each, and no interest was paid on the funds for construction, the house would pay for itself in less than five years, with a gross return on investment of 23 percent per year. A six-room house (which is more common than a four-room house) would yield an even higher rate of return. The 1971 study showed that a government-built NHC house of equivalent size and standards as the "improved" Swahili house would repay its investment at from 11 to 14 percent gross per year. Thus the Swahili house--even with similar features--was twice as good an investment, but its cost was only about 40 percent of the cheapest equivalent NHC house. In addition, the maintenance costs of the Swahili house are probably lower than those for a conventionally built house. A study of Swahili housing in Mombasa (a large coastal town in Kenya with a climate similar to that of Dar es Salaam) reported that--if well maintained--the Swahili house could last indefinitely.[15]

While squatter houseowners in Dar es Salaam tend to live in their own houses, it is common practice to rent rooms to

---

[14]John Leaning, "Low Cost Housing in Tanzania--A Factual Analysis" (Dar es Salaam: Ministry of Lands, Housing and Urban Development, 1971), p. 8.

[15]Saad Yahya, Tradition and Modernity in Residential Investment (University of Nairobi: Department of Land Development, 1971).

lodgers. The larger the house, the larger the proportion of capital investment returned every year. Since bank interest rates have been low and most urban Africans have not been using the banks for their savings, squatter housing has undoubtedly been an important channel for investment in an economic system where there are limited alternative opportunities. If we assume that a medium quality four-room Swahili house cost about Shs. 7,000/- in 1973,[16] and that about 6,000 houses were built in Dar es Salaam in that year, squatter housing involved--at a minimum--a total investment of some Shs. 28 million. This amount is equal to about 47 percent of the total deposits on record with the Tanzania Housing Bank (THB) in mid-1973. The THB was the major source of loan funds for both rural and urban housing throughout the country.

An important reason for building houses for rent is to provide income for the time when one can no longer work. Thus, in discussing the NUMEIST data, Bienefeld says:

> In Tanzania, housing generally played a very important role in terms of social security. In our interviews both with residents of the poorest areas of the cities and with wage earners at their place of work, a constantly recurring theme was the idea that people saved in order to build a . . . house, from which they hoped to rent rooms so as to provide themselves with a steady basic income, especially once they retired.[17]

The dependence on this form of social security is borne out by the NUMEIST data presented in Table 9, which show a steadily increasing proportion of houseownership with age. The figures in Table 9 do not refer to squatter housing only, but the owner-ship pattern indicated there undoubtedly applies at least equally (if not to a greater extent) to squatter housing than to urban housing in general, since squatters tend to be in the lower-in-come groups and thus have fewer formal benefits accruing to them when they retire from employment than do wealthier citizens.[18]

---

[16]Therkildsen and Moriarty, Economic Comparison of Building Materials . . ., p. 11.

[17]M.A. Bienefeld, "The Informal Sector and Peripheral Capital-ism: The Case of Tanzania" (unpublished paper; University of Sussex, Institute of Development Studies, 1974), pp. 14-15.

[18]Houseowners tend to have lived in town for a long time, to be older, and to be Muslim. In Dar es Salaam, Muslims are twice as likely to be houseowners as are Christians, as shown in Table A below. The population of Dar es Salaam in 1967 was 25 percent

Table 9

HOUSEHOLD HEADS/HOUSE OWNERSHIP IN TOWN
IN SEVEN MAIN TOWNS IN TANZANIA, BY AGE: 1971

Age-Group of Household Heads	Proportion in Each Age Group Owning a House in Town	Number in Sample
14-19	1.1%	186
20-24	1.8	598
25-29	6.3	523
30-34	16.3	349
35-39	21.7	309
40-44	28.2	234
45-49	39.1	169
50-59	42.0	200
60 and Over	55.8	147

Source: M.A. Bienefeld, "The Wage Employed," in The National Urban Mobility Employment and Income Survey of Tanzania, Vol. III (Economic Research Bureau, 1972), p. 135.

A final consideration in this discussion of construction costs is the ease with which Swahili houses can be built. Not only is there a large corps of specialized workers available to do the work on different parts of the house, but the building process can be spaced out conveniently according to the owner's pocketbook. The system which has developed in Dar es Salaam is well described in a study prepared by the National Housing and Building Research Unit:

> In former times most houses in Tanzania, including those in the capital, were built by the owner himself, with help from his family and friends. Today many people living in towns prefer to hire fundis [artisans] and labourers to construct their houses. This specialization is one of the inevitable effects of urbanization, and of course, is an important source of wage employment.
> Mud, pole and plaster houses will in general be constructed in the following way. The erection is divided into a number of separate tenders for which the potential house owner can hire various fundis. These will often hire their own labourers if need arises, although the house owner himself can occasionally lend a hand. Erection of poles for walls and roof, application of mud, plastering, flooring, fixing of roof sheets, making the pit and the outhouse etc. can all be separate tenders. Some of these can even be

---

Christian and 67 percent Muslim (Tanzania, Statistical Abstract 1970 [Dar es Salaam, 1972]), which means that the vast majority of houseowners in the city are Muslim. In Dar es Salaam, Muslims undoubtedly have deeper cultural roots and tend to feel more committed to permanent residence. Houseownership reinforces this tendency.

Table A

HOUSE OWNERSHIP BY RELIGION IN DAR ES SALAAM: 1971

Response to Query: Do you own a house in this town?	Religion			
	Christian		Muslim	
	Percent	Number	Percent	Number
No	92%	899	84%	1,803
Yes	8	74	16	332
Totals	100	973	100	2,135

Source: NUMEIST, 1971. Data computed by author.

72

further divided. Up to 9 different fundis might in some
cases be hired for the completion of a house.

During the construction the house owner assumes the role
of organizer. He normally supplies the materials, and
negotiates a price with the various fundis, who are paid
per item produced (blocks) or after completing a definite
part of the house. Payment is withheld until the owner
finds the quality of work satisfactory. However since few
limit themselves to a 7 hour work-day, they probably earn
more than workers on the minimum wage in government service.

The mud pole and plaster construction is easily adapted
to this stage-by-stage approach, and it suits the home-
builder well, since few home-builders can afford to pay for
all the necessary materials and the fundis' wages during a
short period. He can buy the poles and hire a fundi to erect
them. When the potential home owner is satisfied with the
work, he pays the fundi the agreed price. He can now wait
until he has enough money to buy the corrugated iron sheets.
This might take some months, but the poles cannot easily be
removed. After the roof has been finished, the mud is applied to the walls. The house becomes habitable after the
doors and windows have been mounted. When more money is
available the walls can be later improved by plastering (500
sh) and construction of the plinth (300 sh). (By contrast,
in houses with block walls, the initial cost must include
the full cost of the walls and foundations.) Each tender
completes a part of the building. Depending on the financial
situation of the owner the total construction may be spread
over one or even more years.[19]

The System of Compensation. In an effort to meet local
political criticism, the colonial government in Tanganyika--
immediately prior to Independence--established the practice of
paying generous cash compensation to urban squatters who were to
be evicted from land. The basis of payment was the assessed
value of crops and buildings, plus a 50 percent addition as
"disturbance allowance." The "disturbance allowance" has since
been eliminated in favor of giving help to the squatters in resettlement, but the compensation payments for crops and buildings
have continued. Whenever the government wants to move a squatter
from a piece of land, compensation must be paid. The Cabinet
has on several occasions expressed reservations concerning the
principle of cash compensation when alternative surveyed plots
are available, but squatters have steadfastly refused to budge
without compensation. A government study described the system
in 1967 in the following terms:

---

[19]Therkildsen and Moriarty, Economic Comparison of Building
Materials . . ., pp. 14-15. (Emphasis in original.)

The payment of compensation as a means of removing, preventing and controlling unlawful occupation of land and illegal
buildings has been a failure. Where squatters are not provided with an alternative site and directed to it, they move
to another area and later demand further compensation when
being removed. A site that has been cleared by payment of
compensation is soon reoccupied by squatters in the certain
hope of claiming further compensation. When word goes around
that a certain site is to be acquired by Government for urban
or industrial purposes, the number of squatters often re-
doubles overnight.[20]

The amounts paid in compensation have been substantial,
though to obtain precise figures would require a detailed study
of individual disbursements. A rough, and probably conservative,
calculation can be made by totalling government expenditures
under the budgetary items "site clearing and servicing" and
"master plans," and reducing this by 50 percent. From 1964/65
through 1971/72, the Tanzanian government recorded the expenditure of some Shs. 38,326,000 under these headings.[21] Using the
50 percent estimate, this would mean that an average of about
Shs. 2,395,000 per year was spent over the eight-year period
for squatter compensation. The wisdom of the expenditure of
this much money on squatters has been publicly questioned. In
a speech delivered to the annual conference of the Association
of Local Authorities in 1969, the Minister for Lands, Settlement
and Water Development observed:

Squatters are those people who build houses or in any other
way use land in urban centres without the permission of the
Government. They are therefore illegal occupiers and are
in breach of the law. Squatting has reached appalling proportions in many towns in this country but the situation is
particularly and naturally flabbergasting in our capital
city of Dar es Salaam. Squatters are people who have drifted
to the towns for the obvious attractions they offer and
finding it difficult to maintain themselves by renting
houses or rooms, choose some dark corner of the town and
erect their own structures overnight. And they call this
self-reliance! Alternatively, they are people who realise
the shortage of housing in towns and, in order to take advantage of the miseries of town dwellers, erect houses for
renting, charging exhorbitant rents. . . .

[20] Lands Division, "The Problem of Squatters in Urban Areas,"
p. 12.

[21] Ministry of Lands, Housing and Urban Development, Sites and
Services Project, p. 30.

Great and far-reaching disadvantages flow from squatting. . . . Money which could otherwise be used for useful purposes is spent on paying off these squatters when development advances to their strongholds. It might probably be of interest for the Honourable Delegates to learn that it had been estimated to spend Shs. 100,000/- to clear a stretch of five miles for the railway line at Buguruni in Dar es Salaam. On account of the squatters, however, this sum was used to clear only half a mile! Who can tolerate such a situation, I ask you, Honourable Delegates?[22]

The pattern of substantial compensation payments to urban squatters, usually justified on grounds of humanity and expediency, has had at least two notable effects. First, though such payments have been made to only a small minority of the total squatter population, the principle has been established for all squatters that any investment they make in housing will not be lost. With good reason, squatters have assumed that, if evicted, they need only establish a claim to ownership of a house to receive full compensation. A second effect of cash compensation (at least in official minds) has been the creation of a small class of "speculative squatters" who deliberately build in areas where compensation is about to be paid. Since compensation is based on the market value of the materials used in house construction, these "professionals" can realize a profit equal to the cost of the materials they are able to salvage from the compensated house for the purpose of building another house. The return from this form of speculation is, however, as difficult to estimate as it is to prevent.

Policy Implications. As long as economic conditions favor investment in low-cost houses wherever they are built, and compensation payments continue to be made, squatting will remain a profitable economic venture--regardless of the other factors which help to maintain it as an institution in Tanzanian urban life. There is little financial advantage in building on surveyed plots. Under present conditions, surveyed plots are advantageous in comparison with squatter areas only if they are provided with substantially more services than the squatter areas, and are well-located in relation to major places of work-- neither of which is very often the case. The implications of this analysis in policy terms, then, are three:

1. Compensation for those without legal rights of occupancy should be phased out, or the payment schedules considerably reduced in scale;

[22]Speech by the Minister for Lands, Settlement and Water Development to the 12th Annual Conference of the Association of Local Authorities (Dar es Salaam, 1969; mimeo).

2. A great deal more resources should be devoted to servicing high-density areas, either through minimum services or sites and services schemes;

3. Areas close to town but not yet squatter areas should be developed rapidly for low-income occupants.

Unless all three of these courses of action are pursued vigorously and simultaneously, squatting will continue to proliferate in Dar es Salaam.

Chapter IV

SOCIAL AND ECONOMIC CHARACTERISTICS OF
DAR ES SALAAM SQUATTERS

While the history, causes, and physical aspects of squatter development in Dar es Salaam have been analyzed in some
detail, there has been surprisingly little research concerning
the socio-economic characteristics of the squatters themselves.
This type of research is essential, however, because the official
policy response to squatting has heretofore tended to be based
almost entirely on information about the physical conditions of
squatter areas. In the official mind, squatters are generally
seen as mainly poor rural-urban migrants who take advantage of
the government's largesse (and its reluctance to use coercion)
and thereby disrupt programs of planned urban growth which are
in the interests of the whole population. As we saw in the
Introduction to this study, all over the Third World squatting
has been a response to general social and economic features of
developing countries; it cannot be treated as a technical problem
divorced from its context. Tanzania has made a long-range commitment to socialism, but important inequalities persist there--
in both rural and urban society. Squatting reflects certain of
these inequalities. Analysis of the socio-economic characteristics of squatters as compared with non-squatters should bring
out some of the important dimensions of urban inequality in
Tanzania.

The data analyzed in this chapter are derived from the
NUMEIST (National Urban Mobility, Employment and Income Survey
of Tanzania) study, carried out in 1971. The Dar es Salaam
survey responses were separated into two groups, according to
whether the respondents lived in (1) squatter or (2) non-squatter
areas.[1] This grouping procedure was subject to some error, since
the census enumeration areas on which the survey was based were

---

[1] I would like to express my gratitude to M.A. Bienefeld and
R.H. Sabot for giving me access to the raw data from their 1971
survey. Mr. Bienefeld was particularly helpful in sorting
through the Dar es Salaam interviews to distinguish between
those obtained from squatter areas and those from non-squatter
areas. I take full responsibility for the interpretation of the
data provided here.

not always exclusively squatter or non-squatter areas. Internal checks on the data suggest, however, that the groupings were accurate for at least 95 percent of the sample respondents. Since the data base is large (some 3,300 respondents), findings of <u>major</u> differences between squatters and non-squatters would not be affected by minor grouping errors. As long as these major differences found between the squatter and non-squatter groups are analyzed as general patterns, and not in terms of exact magnitudes or as a precise statistical representation of the whole population, no difficulties should arise. In the analysis which follows, "squatters" (as previously defined) are <u>all</u> respondents living in squatter areas of Dar es Salaam--both tenants and landlords. Within the sampled enumeration areas, a random sample of 15 percent of the housing units (houses or individual flats) was selected, within which all adults 14 years of age and over were interviewed using a standard questionnaire.

A. Education and Income

Tanzania is pursuing a strategy aimed at reducing income inequalities both within and between urban and rural areas. The NUMEIST data show that substantial income inequalities exist in the urban population, and that they are closely related to education, which is a <u>structural</u>, rather than a <u>random</u>, basis for inequality. A stratification pattern based on education (however much the differences between top and bottom are reduced) can be expected to continue as long as the increasing bureaucratization of the economy puts a premium on clerical, administrative, and managerial skills. Table 10 presents a cross-tabulation of income and educational levels for the Dar es Salaam sample population, divided into squatter and non-squatter groups. Within both groups, the correlation between income and educational level achieved is <u>very</u> strong. For example, only 4 percent of the squatter respondents and 5 percent of the non-squatter respondents earned an income of Shs. 500/- or more per month; by contrast, virtually all the squatters and 94 percent of the non-squatters with at least Form 5 (some senior secondary) education earned in excess of Shs. 500/- per month. As the level of educational achievement rises, there is a very clear increase in income for both squatters and non-squatters. If educational levels are held constant, however, squatters appear to have earned generally lower incomes than non-squatters. In four of the five educational groups specified in Table 10, a greater proportion of non-squatters than squatters earned over Shs. 500/- per month; the exception is the small "Form 5 and over" group. Not only did squatters generally have less education than non-squatters (see Table 11), but they also appear to have been less able to take advantage of the income opportunities afforded by the education they <u>did</u> receive.

78

Table 10

INCOMES OF SQUATTERS AND NON-SQUATTERS BY EDUCATIONAL LEVELS ACHIEVED: DAR ES SALAAM, 1971

Educational Levels[a]

Monthly Income in Shillings	No Education Squatters		No Education Non-Squatters		Standards 1-4 Squatters		Standards 1-4 Non-Squatters		Standards 5-8 Squatters		Standards 5-8 Non-Squatters		Forms 1-4 Squatters		Forms 1-4 Non-Squatters		Forms 5-6 and University Squatters		Forms 5-6 and University Non-Squatters	
	Per-cent	N[b]	Per-cent	N	Per-cent	N	Per-cent	N	Per-cent	N	Per-cent	N	Per-cent	N	Per-cent	N	Per-cent	N	Per-cent	N
1-99/-	15%	45	15%	14	11%	23	6%	7	5%	13	1%	3	2%	1	--	--	--	--	--	--
100-199/-	31	91	17	16	27	56	22	24	16	42	13	29	10	6	1	1	--	--	--	--
200-299/-	31	91	43	40	36	76	31	34	42	109	32	74	21	13	9	13	--	--	--	--
300-399/-	14	41	18	17	18	38	16	17	20	51	22	50	14	9	18	28	--	--	3	1
400-499/-	4	11	1	1	5	11	8	9	7	19	11	25	6	4	7	10	--	--	3	1
500-749/-	3	10	3	3	1	2	9	10	7	19	10	22	27	17	26	40	44	4	17	5
750-999/-	--	--	--	--	1	2	--	--	1	2	4	8	10	6	10	15	--	--	7	2
1000-1499/-	1	4	--	--	<1	1	1	1	<1	1	3	7	2	1	16	25	22	2	23	7
1500/- and up	<1	1	2	2	1	2	6	6	1	2	4	10	10	6	13	20	33	3	47	14
Totals	99	294	99	93	100	211	99	108	99	258	100	228	102	63	100	152	99	9	100	30

Grand Total N: 1,446

[a] Educational Levels

Standards 1-4 = 1-4 years
Standards 5-8 = 5-8 years
Forms 1-4 = 9-12 years
Forms 5-6 = 13-14 years
University = 17 years or over

[b] N = Number of respondents.

Table 11

LEVELS OF FORMAL EDUCATION ACHIEVED BY SQUATTERS AND
NON-SQUATTERS: DAR ES SALAAM, 1971

Level of Education[a]	Squatters		Non-Squatters	
	Percent	Number	Percent	Number
No formal education	50%	924	28%	392
Standards 1-4	21	396	18	249
Standards 5-8	23	434	31	440
Forms 1-4	5	100	21	291
Forms 5-6	--	7	1	23
University	--	4	1	22
Totals	99	1,865	100	1,417

[a]For explanation, see note a in Table 10.

B. Religion

        In terms of access to economic rewards in Tanzania,
religion is an important factor because of its strong historical
relationship to education. During the colonial period, Christians
were much more likely than Muslims (or pagans) to have attended
school. In general, men were better educated than women, but
the differences between the sexes were much less pronounced
among Christians than among Muslims.[2] The NUMEIST data have
not been organized in this study to provide a male/female breakdown, but the overall past association between education and
religion seems to have continued to the present. Table 12 presents the survey data showing the relation between religion
and education for the squatter population in Dar es Salaam in
1971. The figures in this table indicate that Christians were
more than twice as likely to have attended school as Muslims,
and seven times as likely to have completed some secondary
school education.

        In terms of the religious affiliation of respondents,
there are no great differences between squatter and non-squatter
areas in Dar es Salaam. In the 1971 sample, Muslims were slightly underrepresented in the non-squatter areas and slightly
overrepresented in the squatter areas, as measured against
1967 census figures. The somewhat heavier representation of
Muslims in the squatter areas is probably accounted for largely
by the high percentage of coastal people living in the original
villages absorbed by the city.

C. Houseownership

        There are substantial differences in the pattern of
houseownership between squatter and non-squatter areas in Dar

---

[2]The relationships among religion, education, and sex in
colonial Tanganyika are shown in these figures from the 1957
African census:

Religion	Percentage of African Population Ever Attended School	
	Male	Female
Protestant	36.9%	20.2%
Roman Catholic	34.4	19.0
Islam	18.0	4.0
Pagan and other	7.9	2.0

Source: Tanganyika, African Census Report, 1957, p. 72.

Table 12

EDUCATIONAL ACHIEVEMENT BY RELIGIOUS AFFILIATION
OF DAR ES SALAAM SQUATTERS: 1971

| Highest Educational Level Achieved[a] | Religious Affiliation | | | |
| | Muslim | | Christian | |
	Percent	Number	Percent	Number
None	62%	799	20%	105
Standards 1-4	17	220	31	161
Standards 5-8	19	244	34	179
Forms 1-4	2	26	13	70
Forms 5-6 and University	--	2	1	7
Totals	100	1,286	99	522

[a]For explanation, see note a in Table 10.

82

es Salaam. Table 13 shows that 17 percent of the adults surveyed
in the squatter areas in 1971 were houseowners, compared to only
7 percent in the planned areas. The survey also shows that very
few houseowners in the squatter areas owned more than one house
in 1971, which seems to be a clear indication that these houseowners were living in their own houses; in other words, there
appears to have been little or no absentee houseownership.
Other survey tabulations show that houseowners' total income
in 1971 did not differ significantly from the income of tenants,
in both the squatter and non-squatter areas. Whatever the major
factors were in income differentiation in Dar es Salaam, houseownership was not one of them.

In the preceding discussion of house construction (p. 70,
fn. 18 above), we saw that Muslims in Dar es Salaam were twice
as likely to be houseowners as Christians. In Table 14, the
religious percentages for houseownership are broken down for
squatter and non-squatter areas. While in squatter areas Muslims
were roughly twice as likely to be houseowners as Christians, in
non-squatter areas they were three times as likely to be houseowners. This probably reflected the fact that the Muslim African
population in Dar es Salaam had (on the whole) lived longer in
the city than the Christian, and thus had had the opportunity
over a longer time to find housing in the planned areas.

D. Migrant/Non-Migrant

Migration from rural areas in Tanzania accounts for the
larger part of the population growth in Dar es Salaam. To what
extent are these migrants forced to seek housing in squatter
areas? With the data available we cannot answer this question
directly; however, we can classify the survey respondents as
either "migrants" or "non-migrants." A "migrant" is defined
as anyone who came to Dar es Salaam after the age of thirteen.
When this definition is used, we find that migrants are only
slightly more likely to be living in squatter areas than in
non-squatter areas (see Table 15). This finding throws considerable doubt on the presumption that there is a one-to-one
relationship between heavy rural-urban migration and proliferation of squatter settlements.

The relationships between migration and squatting can
be further analyzed using the tabulations from the NUMEIST survey
data provided in Tables 16, 17, and 18, which compare squatters
and non-squatters with respect to their reasons for coming to
Dar es Salaam, their fathers' occupations, and their rights to
land in their home areas.

1. Reasons for Coming to Dar es Salaam. The migrants
who come to Dar es Salaam do so for many different reasons. In

Table 13

HOUSEOWNERSHIP BY SQUATTER AND NON-SQUATTER AREAS
IN DAR ES SALAAM: 1971

Answer to Query: Do you own a house in this town?	Squatter Areas		Non-Squatter Areas	
	Percent	Number	Percent	Number
No	83%	1,552	93%	1,317
Yes	17	320	7	99
Totals	100	1,872	100	1,416

Table 14

HOUSEHOWNERSHIP BY RELIGIOUS AFFILIATION IN SQUATTER AND NON-SQUATTER AREAS:
DAR ES SALAAM, 1971

Answer to Query: Do you own a house in this town?	Religious Affiliation							
	Christian				Muslim			
	Squatter Areas		Non-Squatter Areas		Squatter Areas		Non-Squatter Areas	
	Percent	Number	Percent	Number	Percent	Number	Percent	Number
No	89%	464	97%	435	81%	1,040	90%	763
Yes	11	60	3	14	19	251	10	81
Totals	100	524	100	449	100	1,291	100	844

Table 15

MIGRANT/NON-MIGRANT STATUS BY SQUATTER AND NON-SQUATTER
AREAS IN DAR ES SALAAM: 1971

Migrant Status	Squatter Areas		Non-Squatter Areas	
	Percent	Number	Percent	Number
Migrant	69%	1,295	66%	932
Non-Migrant	31	578	34	488
Totals	100	1,873	100	1,320

Table 16, the reasons for migration given by samples of migrants
living in squatter and non-squatter areas in 1971 are broken
down by percentages. Significantly more non-squatters than
squatters came to the capital city to go to school, because of
job transfers, or to take jobs obtained before coming. By contrast, more squatters than non-squatters came to Dar es Salaam
to look for work.

2. Father's Occupation. In combination with data on
education and income, data on fathers' occupations help us to
determine the class composition of the squatter and non-squatter
populations in Dar es Salaam. In Table 17, six categories of
fathers' occupations are listed for both squatters and non-
squatters (further divided into migrants and non-migrants).
Some striking differences between squatters and non-squatters
are shown. For example, squatters are much more likely than
non-squatters to have fathers who are peasants, and less likely
to have fathers who are professionals/civil servants or business-
men/traders. Thus, while the class background of both squatters
and non-squatters is predominantly rural peasant, that of non-
squatters is better balanced between peasant and urban middle
class. As migrants establish themselves in the town, there is
a consistent movement away from a peasant background toward an
urban middle-class background. In Table 17, the biggest differences in class background are between squatter migrants
(fathers 86 percent peasant and 8 percent professional/business)
and non-squatter non-migrants (fathers 40 percent peasant and
31 percent professional/business). To a considerable extent,
then, living in squatter areas (particularly for migrants) is a
reflection of both class background and class position.

3. Access to Rural Land. The degree to which urban
dwellers have lost free access to rural land in their home areas
is a measure of their urban involvement. Because there are few
rural areas with land shortages in Tanzania, most of the migrant
urban population still has access to rural land. However, as
is shown in Table 18, there is substantial difference in land
access between squatters and non-squatters. One-third of the
non-squatter population, compared to one-sixth of the squatters,
claim they have no rights to land in the rural areas. This is
consistent with the differences in class background and position
discussed above, and further illustrates the rural peasant
orientation of the squatter population.

Within the squatter population, there are two additional
dimensions related to migration. Presumably the same relationships obtain for non-squatters, but the confirming data are not
available. First, there is a very strong relationship between
religion and migrant status. Christians are much more likely
to be migrants than are Muslims; conversely, Muslims are almost
three times as likely to be non-migrants (i.e., permanent urban

Table 16

REASONS FOR MIGRATION TO DAR ES SALAAM
OF SQUATTERS AND NON-SQUATTERS: 1971

Reason for Migration[a]	Squatters		Non-Squatters	
	Percent	Number	Percent	Number
Government transfer[b]	2%	30	3%	40
Employer transfer[b]	1	17	2	24
To attend school[b]	3	50	6	90
To take job obtained prior to migration[b]	2	43	4	53
To look for work[b]	24	439	19	269
To accompany parents	17	309	16	230
To accompany husband	23	428	20	281
To visit	10	181	9	122
Other	5	97	4	58
Don't know/Not stated	14	255	17	239
Totals	101	1,849	100	1,416

[a]More than one response possible.

[b]Significant difference between percentages of squatters and non-squatters.

Table 17

FATHERS' OCCUPATIONS OF DAR ES SALAAM SQUATTERS AND NON-SQUATTERS (MIGRANTS/NON-MIGRANTS): 1971

| | Squatters | | | | Non-Squatters | | | |
| | Migrants | | Non-Migrants | | Migrants | | Non-Migrants | |
Father's Occupation	Percent	Number	Percent	Number	Percent	Number	Percent	Number
Peasant/farmer	86%	1,002	67%	348	69%	598	40%	164
Professional (teacher, manager/administration/service)	6	67	8	40	10	87	11	47
Clerical/sales	1	14	2	8	2	18	7	28
Skilled/semi-skilled	5	54	12	62	6	48	17	72
Unskilled	1	9	10	52	1	6	5	20
Business/trade	2	19	3	13	12	103	20	83
Totals	101	1,165	102	518	100	860	100	414

Table 18

RIGHTS TO LAND IN RURAL HOME AREAS HELD BY DAR ES SALAAM MIGRANTS: 1971

| | Squatters | | Non-Squatters | |
Answer to Query: If you went back home, would there be land for you?	Percent	Number	Percent	Number
Yes	83%	983	67%	577
No	17	198	33	286
Totals	100	1,181	100	863

residents) as are Christians. Second, migrants are considerably less likely to be houseowners than are non-migrants. (It will be recalled that Muslims are much more likely to be houseowners than are Christians.)

In the light of data we have presented concerning the relations of education/religion/migration, it appears that two relatively distinct life-styles have emerged in Dar es Salaam: these might be called the "coastal Muslim" and the "up-country Christian" styles. Those in the "coastal Muslim" group tend to have little formal education, to have lived much or all of their lives in and around Dar es Salaam, and to be houseowners. Those in the "up-country Christian" group generally have five or more years of formal education, are migrants to the city, and are not houseowners. The two life-styles parallel both class and institutional differentiation, since Christian migrants (because of their superior education) have tended to obtain most of the higher-paying jobs in the bureaucracy, while older, mainly Muslim residents have traditionally controlled TANU in Dar es Salaam. It is at least arguable that the continuing conflicts between TANU and the bureaucracy have in part been a reflection of the divergences between these two life-styles.

E. Occupation and Income

1. Occupation. As might be expected, educational differences between squatters and non-squatters tend to be reflected in different occupational profiles for the two groups. Table 19, which gives a rough occupational breakdown, shows that squatters are more likely to be self-employed or engaged in casual and wage labor than are non-squatters. Squatters are not significantly more likely to be unemployed than non-squatters. Non-squatters, on the other hand, show significantly higher proportions of salaried staff and senior management. This occupational profile appears to be related to the different types of employers for the two groups. The data in Table 20 indicate that--among employees--squatters tend to work more for private employers than do non-squatters, while non-squatters tend to work more for parastatals (which often provide employee housing) and the central government. The squatter areas often have bustling local building industries and a proliferation of small-scale trading establishments--indeed a wide range of enterprise that is either irrelevant to, or inappropriate to, the planned areas. Examples of such enterprise are building-related crafts (e.g., making door and window frames), selling mangrove poles and other Swahili-type building supplies, water carrying, and growing fruits and vegetables for sale.

2. Income. The income data provided by the NUMEIST study are organized in three categories: non-wage income, wage

90

Table 19

EMPLOYMENT STATUS OF SQUATTERS AND NON-SQUATTERS
IN DAR ES SALAAM: 1971[a]

	Squatters		Non-Squatters	
Employment Status	Percent	Number	Percent	Number
Kibarua/casual	9%	128	5%	49
Regular wage	26	351	19	183
Salaried staff	21	289	38	379
Senior management	--	4	2	15
Self-employed/non-wage	21	294	16	161
Unemployed or seeking work	22	309	20	197
Totals	99	1,375	100	984

[a]This table is based upon answers to two separate (but over-lapping) questions, and must be interpreted with care. The category "Unemployed or seeking work" refers to all those who answered that they were seeking work; it overlaps somewhat with other categories. Also, the term "regular wage" has not been used consistently.

Table 20

TYPES OF EMPLOYERS OF SQUATTER AND NON-SQUATTER
WAGE-EARNERS IN DAR ES SALAAM: 1971

Type of Employer	Squatters		Non-Squatters	
	Percent	Number	Percent	Number
Private firm	35%	266	28%	173
Private individual	8	61	5	33
Government	23	177	25	157
Parastatal	34	263	41	257
Other	--	1	--	2
Totals	100	768	99	622

income, and total income (wage + non-wage). (In general, questions relating to income are among those having the lowest rate
of response in survey studies.) These data are tabulated for
individuals (both men and women)--not households.[3]

The survey data on non-wage income are presented in
Table 21. As would be expected, there are proportionately more
squatters than non-squatters in the non-wage group, but it is
interesting to note that the average income earned by non-squatters in this group appears to be somewhat higher than that earned
by squatters. (This may be due in part to the number of Asian
shopkeepers included in the non-wage group.) In any case, 45
percent of the non-squatters in the non-wage group earned an
income of over Shs. 300/- per month, while only 20 percent of
the squatters earned that amount. Almost one quarter of the
non-squatters earned incomes in the highest range (Shs. 1500/-
per month and over), while only 2 percent of the squatters were
in this category.[4]

The figures for wage income are shown in Table 22. Wage
income is much more important than non-wage income in terms of
the number of people covered. It is easier for people to recall
their monthly wage than to estimate their non-wage income, which
makes it probable that a relatively high proportion of the survey
responses concerning wage incomes are valid. The figures show
a significant difference between squatters and non-squatters.
While 85 percent of squatter wage-earners earned less than Shs.
400/- per month in 1971, the corresponding proportion for non-
squatters was 58 percent. (Stated conversely, only 15 percent
of squatter wage-earners earned Shs. 400/- or more per month,
while 42 percent of non-squatter wage-earners earned Shs. 400/-
or more.)

The figures for total income (shown in Table 23) tell
much the same story as those for wage income. The proportions
of both squatters and non-squatters earning less than Shs. 400/-

---

[3]To determine household income, it would be necessary to
multiply the tabulations by a factor representing the assumed
difference between household and individual incomes.

[4]A detailed analysis of all non-wage earners in the national
sample has been carried out by Bienefeld as part of a study of
the interrelationships between the informal sector and peripheral
capitalism. For a presentation of the analysis and the basic
data, see M.A. Bienefeld, "The Self-Employed of Urban Tanzania,"
I.D.S. Discussion Paper No. 54 (University of Sussex, 1974).
The implications drawn from these data are analyzed in Bienefeld,
"The Informal Sector and Peripheral Capitalism. . . ."

Table 21

NON-WAGE INCOMES OF SQUATTERS AND NON-SQUATTERS
IN DAR ES SALAAM: 1971

Monthly Income in Shillings	Squatters		Non-Squatters	
	Percent	Number	Percent	Number
1-99/-	36%	64	20%	18
100-199/-	27	49	24	22
200-299/-	16	28	10	9
300-399/-	8	15	8	7
400-499/-	3	6	4	4
500-749/-	4	7	4	4
750-999/-	--	1	2	2
1000-1499/-	3	6	3	3
1500/- and over	2	3	24	22
Totals	99	179	99	91

Table 22

DISTRIBUTION OF WAGE INCOME BY SQUATTER, NON-SQUATTER,
AND TOTAL AREAS IN DAR ES SALAAM: 1971

Monthly Wage in Shillings	Squatter Areas		Non-Squatter Areas		Total Area	
	Percent	Number	Percent	Number	Percent	Number
1-99/-	6%	39	1%	8	4%	47
100-199/-	23	162	10	57	17	219
200-299/-	38	269	28	154	34	423
300-399/-	18	128	19	103	18	231
400-499/-	5	38	8	42	6	80
500-749/-	6	42	14	78	9	120
750-999/-	1	9	5	25	3	34
1000-1499/-	--	3	8	44	4	47
1500/- and over	2	11	7	40	4	51
Totals	99	701	100	551	99	1,252

Table 23

DISTRIBUTION OF TOTAL INCOME (WAGE + NON-WAGE) BY
SQUATTER, NON-SQUATTER, AND TOTAL AREAS IN
DAR ES SALAAM: 1971

Monthly Income in Shillings	Squatter Areas		Non-Squatter Areas		Total Area	
	Percent	Number	Percent	Number	Percent	Number
1-99/-	10%	84	4%	23	7%	107
100-199/-	24	200	11	71	18	271
200-299/-	34	291	26	163	31	454
300-399/-	17	144	18	112	17	256
400-499/-	5	45	8	47	6	92
500-749/-	6	53	13	81	9	134
750-999/-	1	10	4	28	3	38
1000-1499/-	1	9	7	46	4	55
1500/- and over	2	14	9	59	5	73
Totals	100	850	100	630	100	1,480

and Shs. 400/- and more are about the same as when wage incomes alone are considered. However, the inclusion of a fairly sizable group of non-wage income respondents--some of whom earned very little indeed--has lowered the distribution of income in the "less than Shs. 400/- per month" category to the point that 34 percent of the squatters and 15 percent of the non-squatters had incomes of less than Shs. 200/- per month in 1971.

F. Rent

We would expect rental patterns in squatter and non-squatter areas to be very different. In the squatter areas, 76 percent of renters paid less than Shs. 30/- per month for rent in 1971; the corresponding proportion for renters in the non-squatter areas was only 22 percent. The modal rent in the squatter areas was Shs. 25/-, while in the non-squatter areas it was Shs. 35/-. Almost one quarter (23 percent) of the non-squatters paid rents of Shs. 50/- or more, compared to only 10 percent of the squatters. Clearly the difference in rent structures is a strong incentive to reside in squatter areas, despite the generally very low level of services provided.

A second difference between rental patterns in squatter and non-squatter areas is that rentals in squatter areas are very predominantly (89 percent) for single rooms only, while in the non-squatter areas the predominance of single room rentals is somewhat less--76 percent. Assuming that people who rent in squatter areas do so primarily because the rents are lower, this seems to indicate that very few are prepared to pay more rent in order to have more space and/or better services.

In sum, the data discussed in this chapter reinforce our initial impression that urban squatting is a reflection of persisting inequalities in Tanzanian society as a whole. While some of these inequalities (such as those relating to income) may have been diminished over time by the determined application of socialist measures, others (such as those relating to formal education) may loom even larger as keys to access to benefits in an increasingly powerful public sector. In terms of an overall comparison of the squatter population of Dar es Salaam to the non-squatter population, the NUMEIST survey data show that squatters in general are more likely (1) to have lower incomes, (2) to own their own houses or, if renters, to pay lower rents and rent fewer rooms, (3) to have come from peasant families, (4) to have migrated to town to look for work, (5) to have maintained rights to rural land, and (6) to be employed in the "informal sector" earning a non-wage income. On the other hand, squatters are not necessarily more likely to be rural-urban migrants, and there is no pronounced religious difference between squatters and non-squatters.

In Tanzania today, most of the contrasts we have observed are strongly linked to levels of formal education achieved. Significantly, one of the most marked differences between squatters and non-squatters is in education. Since squatters as a group have much less formal education than non-squatters, their access to a wide range of urban occupations and facilities is much more limited. For example, those without good educational qualifications cannot get secure, well-paid jobs in the formal institutional sector. These jobs tend to carry with them access to subsidized modern housing, medical and retirement benefits, and "contacts" in the bureaucratic structure which are of inestimable value in obtaining scarce goods, information, and even job opportunities for relatives and friends. Urban squatters, because of their tremendous social and occupational heterogeneity, are not collectively a class--either subjectively or objectively; but squatters as individuals are disadvantaged by class factors in the larger society. In a situation where a poor, predominantly rural country can devote few of its scarce resources to an already privileged urban sector, it is probably inevitable that inequalities within the urban sector--as reflected in the size and growth of the squatter population--will be almost impossible to eradicate.

Chapter V

SUMMARY AND CONCLUSIONS

The growth of squatting in urban Tanzania, as in many
other Third World countries, can be analyzed in part as a
technical problem in planning, but its basic causes lie much
deeper, and to bring it to an end will require far-reaching and
profound solutions.

As a technical problem, squatting in the main towns of
Tanzania is an increasingly severe constraint on orderly planning.
Proper services cannot be provided to squatter areas, health
standards are becoming more difficult to maintain, and the land
occupied by squatters cannot be put to its optimum use. Some
squatting has always been associated with urbanization in Tanzania, but there has been an alarming increase in the number of
squatters since the period immediately prior to Independence.
Between 1969 and 1972, the squatter areas of Dar es Salaam
grew at an average yearly rate of 24 percent, to the point that
by 1972 squatters constituted about 44 percent of the population
of the capital city. Among the major factors contributing to
this growth are (1) the inability of the various government
agencies concerned with land use to carry out their legal re-
sponsibilities with respect to unauthorized occupation of public
land, and (2) the economic advantages of squatting.

Over the years, many different attempts have been made
to deal with the squatter problem in Tanzania, and urban policy
has been moving steadily toward greater assistance for the lower-
income groups in the population. Judging by the increase in
squatting, however, the total impact of both the individual
initiatives undertaken and the overall urban policy has been
negligible.

The analysis presented in this study suggests which technical approaches to the problem of squatting are likely to be
more (or less) effective than others. For example, the "slum
clearance and/or relocation" approach would probably be the most
costly and the least beneficial for the people immediately affected. Squatters are too dependent (our data show) on neigh-
borhood-level, non-wage income for their livelihood. Not only
would relocation disrupt this pattern, but also their incomes
are not sufficient for them to either buy or rent new, NHC-type
housing. However, our analysis shows that only very vigorous
action will discourage squatting, and that the overall problem

99

probably cannot be eliminated without major structural change. A great deal more money will have to be found for servicing high-density surveyed areas (either through minimal-services or sites and services schemes, or a combination of both); areas close to the towns which are not yet squatter areas will have to be developed rapidly; compensation payments to squatters will have to be phased out. This three-pronged program--if pursued in a coordinated and energetic fashion--should substantially reduce the economic incentives to squatting, making it unnecessary for the government to use force to achieve planned urban development.

Even the success of this program, however, will depend on a generally supportive context. As we have attempted to show, squatting in Tanzania is the result of a series of historical, social, and institutional factors which have produced an urban social system characterized by significant inequalities. In terms of the income differential between the top and the bottom, these inequalities are now much less than they were at Independence, but in a country planning for socialism, the differential which remains is still unacceptable. Of course, squatting is only one reflection of social and economic inequalities; it will persist, however, so long as Tanzania can devote only very limited resources to urban development. For squatting to be significantly reduced, rural-urban migration would have to be slowed down considerably (which would presuppose an effective large-scale program of rural development and the reduction of the urban-rural income differential), the central government bureaucracy would have to be made much more efficient than it now is, and greatly increased resources would have to be made available for urban planning.

Any increase in the allocation of scarce public resources to the urban sector in Tanzania raises the question of political will in a society that is over 90 percent rural and a state where representative institutions are controlled by a mass, rural-based political party. The tension between the need to develop the rural areas and the legitimate claims of lower-income groups in the urban areas is clearly shown in the writings of President Nyerere. The 1967 Arusha Declaration (which Nyerere drafted) includes a strong warning to Tanzanians against the unrestricted development of the towns:

We must not forget that people who live in towns can possibly become the exploiters of those who live in the rural areas. All our big hospitals are in towns and they benefit only a small section of the people of Tanzania. Yet if we have built them with loans from outside Tanzania, it is the overseas sale of the peasants' produce which provides the foreign exchange for repayment. . . . Tarmac roads, too, are mostly found in towns and are of especial value to the motor-car

owners. . . . Again, electric lights, water pipes, hotels
and other aspects of modern development are mostly found in
towns. Most of them have been built with loans, and most
of them do not benefit the farmer directly, although they
will be paid for by the foreign exchange earned by the sale
of his produce. We should always bear this in mind.[1]

Later in the same year, however, in the important paper "Socialism
and Rural Development," Nyerere was careful to qualify the views
he had expressed earlier, which seemed to imply that all urban
dwellers lived a privileged existence. He restated his position
thus:

[T]here is an almost universal belief that life in the towns
is more comfortable and more secure--that the rewards of
work are better in the urban areas and that people in the
rural parts of the country are condemned to poverty and in-
security for their whole lives.
But although the goal of individual wealth has been
accepted by our people, and despite their belief that this
can be attained by wage employment and by life in the towns,
the truth is that it is an unrealistic goal, especially in
Tanzania. The vast majority even of our town dwellers live
extremely poorly, and in most cases they are on the whole
worse off, both materially and in the realm of personal
satisfaction, than the people in the rural areas could be.
An unskilled worker in the towns or on the agricultural
estates earns wages which are hardly sufficient to enable
a family to eat a proper diet and live in a decent house.[2]

The attempt to resolve these two views has been a common
thread running through Tanzanian urban policy proposals since
the late 1960's. Hopefully, urban development planning in the
1970's will creatively translate the policy dilemma these views
present into programs which will effectively ameliorate the
living conditions of the urban poor.

---

[1] Julius K. Nyerere, Ujamaa: Essays on Socialism (Dar es Salaam:
Oxford University Press, 1968), pp. 27-28.

[2] Ibid., pp. 111-12.

BIBLIOGRAPHY

Books and Articles

Abrams, Charles. Man's Struggle for Shelter in an Urbanizing World. Cambridge, Mass.: M.I.T. Press, 1966.

Barioch, Paul. Urban Unemployment in Developing Countries. Geneva: International Labour Organization, 1973.

Berry, L., ed. Tanzania in Maps. London: University of London Press, 1971.

Bienefeld, Manfred A. The Wage Employed. The National Urban Mobility, Employment and Income Survey of Tanzania, Volume III. University of Dar es Salaam: Economic Research Bureau, 1972.

_____. "The Informal Sector and Peripheral Capitalism: The Case of Tanzania." Unpublished paper. University of Sussex, Institute of Development Studies, 1974.

_____. "The Self-Employed of Urban Tanzania." I.D.S. Discussion Paper No. 54. University of Sussex, 1974.

_____, and Binhammer, Helmuth H. "Tanzania Housing Finance and Housing Policy." In John Hutton, ed., Urban Challenge in East Africa. Nairobi: East African Publishing House, 1972.

BRALUP (Bureau of Resource Assessment and Land Use Planning of the University of Dar es Salaam). See under Claeson.

Breese, Gerald, ed. The City in Newly Developing Countries. Englewood Cliffs: Prentice-Hall, 1969.

Brown, Walter T. "Bagamoyo: An Historical Introduction," Tanzania Notes and Records, 71 (1970), pp. 69-83.

Byerlee, Derek. Research on Migration in Africa: Past Present and Future. African Rural Employment Study: Rural Employment Paper No. 2. Department of Agricultural Economics, Michigan State University, September 1972.

_____, and Eicher, Carl K. Rural Employment, Migration and

Economic Development: Theoretical Issues and Empirical Evidence from Africa. African Rural Employment Study: Rural Employment Paper No. 1. Department of Agricultural Economics, Michigan State University, September 1972.

Chenery, Hollis, et al. *Redistribution with Growth.* London: Oxford University Press, 1974.

Claeson, Claes-Fredrik, and Egero, Bertil. *Migration and the Urban Population: A Demographic Analysis of Population Census Data for Tanzania.* University of Dar es Salaam: BRALUP Research Notes No. 11:2, 1972.

_____, and _____. *Migration in Tanzania: A Review Based on the 1967 Population Census.* University of Dar es Salaam: BRALUP Research Notes No. 11:3, 1972.

_____, and _____. *Movement to Towns in Tanzania: Tables and Comments.* University of Dar es Salaam: BRALUP Research Notes No. 11:1, 1971.

Cliffe, Lionel, and Cunningham, Griffiths. "Ideology, Organisation and the Settlement Experience in Tanzania." In L. Cliffe and John Saul, eds., *Socialism in Tanzania,* Vol. II. Nairobi: East African Publishing House, 1973.

_____, and Saul, John, eds. *Socialism in Tanzania,* Vol. II. Nairobi: East African Publishing House, 1973.

Clinard, Marshall. *Slums and Community Development: Experiments in Self-Help.* New York: The Free Press, 1966.

Currie, Lauchlin. "The Colombian Plan 1971-1974: A Test of the Leading Sector Strategy," *World Development,* Vol. 2, Nos. 10-12 (October/December 1974), pp. 69-72.

Cohen, Robin, and Michael, David. "The Revolutionary Potential of the African Lumpenproletariat: A Sceptical View," *Bulletin.* University of Sussex, Institute of Development Studies, Vol. 5, No. 2/3 (October 1973), pp. 31-42.

Cornelius, Wayne A., Jr. "Urbanization as an Agent in Latin American Political Instability: The Case of Mexico," *American Political Science Review,* Vol. 63, No. 3 (September 1969), pp. 833-57.

Daily Nation (Nairobi), 1 December 1972; 2 October 1973.

Daily News (Dar es Salaam), 14 February 1973.

East African Standard (Nairobi), 28 September 1972.

Elkan, Walter. "Is a Proletariat Emerging in Nairobi?" University of Nairobi: Institute for Development Studies, Discussion Paper, 1972.

Employment in Africa: Some Critical Issues. Geneva: International Labour Office, 1973.

Employment, Incomes and Equality: A Strategy for Increasing Productive Employment in Kenya. Geneva: International Labour Office, 1972.

Fanon, Frantz. The Wretched of the Earth. Harmondsworth: Penguin, 1967.

Frank, C.R., Jr. "Urban Unemployment and Economic Growth in Africa," Oxford Economic Papers (New Series), Vol. 20 (July 1968).

Friedmann, John, and Sullivan, Flora. "The Absorption of Labor in the Urban Economy: The Case of Developing Countries," Economic Development and Cultural Change, Vol. 22, No. 3 (April 1974), pp. 385-413.

Green, Reginald H. "Tanzania." In H. Chenery et al., Redistribution with Growth. London: Oxford University Press, 1974.

Grohs, Gerhard. "Slum Clearance in Dar es Salaam." In John Hutton, ed., Urban Challenge in East Africa. Nairobi: East African Publishing House, 1972.

Gugler, Josef. "On the Theory of Rural-Urban Migration: The Case of Subsaharan Africa." In J.A. Jackson, ed., Migration. Cambridge: Cambridge University Press, 1969. [Sociological Studies: 2]

_____, ed. Urban Growth in Subsaharan Africa. Kampala: Makerere University, 1969.

Gulliver, P.H. Labour Migration in a Rural Economy. Kampala: East African Institute of Social Research, 1955.

Gutkind, Peter C.W. The Emergent African Urban Proletariat. Montreal: McGill University, Centre for Developing-Area Studies, 1974. [Occasional Paper No. 8]

Harris, John R., and Todaro, Michael P. "Migration, Unemployment and Development: A Two-Sector Analysis," The American Economic Review, Vol. 60, No. 1, pp. 126-42.

Helleiner, G.K. "Socialism and Economic Development in Tanzania," Journal of Development Studies, Vol. 8, No. 2 (January 1972), pp. 183-204.

BIBLIOGRAPHY

Hutton, Caroline. Reluctant Farmers? A Study of Unemployment and Planned Rural Development in Uganda. Nairobi: East African Publishing House, 1973.

Hutton, John, ed. Urban Challenge in East Africa. Nairobi: East African Publishing House, 1972.

Iliffe, John. "The Age of Improvement and Differentiation (1907-45)." In I.N. Kimambo and A.J. Temu, eds., A History of Tanzania. Nairobi: East African Publishing House, 1969.

International Labour Office. Report to the Government of the United Republic of Tanzania on Wages, Incomes and Prices Policy. Government Paper No. 3, 1967. Dar es Salaam: Government Printer, 1967.

Jackson, J.A., ed. Migration. Cambridge: Cambridge University Press, 1969. [Sociological Studies: 2]

James, R.W. Land Tenure and Policy in Tanzania. Nairobi: East African Literature Bureau, 1971.

Kimambo, I.N., and Temu, A.J., eds. A History of Tanzania. Nairobi: East African Publishing House, 1969.

Laquian, Aprodicio A. Rural-Urban Migrants and Metropolitan Development. Toronto: Methuen Publications for INTERMET, 1971.

Leaning, John. "Housing and Land Distribution in Tanzania." Dar es Salaam: Ministry of Lands, Housing and Urban Development, 1971.

_____. "Low Cost Housing in Tanzania--A Factual Analysis." Dar es Salaam: Ministry of Lands, Housing and Urban Development, 1971.

_____. "Squatter Housing in Dar es Salaam." Dar es Salaam: Ministry of Lands, Housing and Urban Development, 1972.

Lerner, Daniel. "Comparative Analysis of Processes of Modernisation." In Horace Miner, ed., The City in Modern Africa. London: Pall Mall Press, 1967.

Leslie, J.A.K. A Survey of Dar es Salaam. London: Oxford University Press, 1963.

Levine, Ned. "The Revolutionary Non-Potential of the 'Lumpen': Essence or Technical Deficiency?," Bulletin. University of Sussex, Institute of Development Studies, Vol. 5, No. 2/3 (October 1973), pp. 43-52.

BIBLIOGRAPHY

Leys, Colin. "Interpreting African Underdevelopment: Reflections on the ILO Report on Employment, Incomes and Equality in Kenya," _African Affairs_, Vol. 72 (October 1973).

Mangin, William. "Latin American Squatter Settlements: A Problem and a Solution," _Latin American Research Review_, Summer 1967.

Marris, Peter. _Family and Social Change in an African City_. Evanston: Northwestern University Press, 1961.

Mascarenhas, Adolfo C. "Urban Centres." In L. Berry, ed., _Tanzania in Maps_. London: University of London Press, 1971.

_____, and Claeson, C.-F. "Factors Influencing Tanzania's Urban Policy," _African Urban Notes_, Vol. 6, No. 3 (Fall 1972).

McGee, T.G. _The Southeast Asian City_. London: G. Bell and Sons, 1967.

Meier, Gerald M., ed. _Leading Issues in Development Economics_. New York: Oxford University Press, 1964.

Miliband, Ralph, and Saville, John, eds. _The Socialist Register 1972_. London: Merlin Press, 1972.

Mkama, J. "Urban Development Policies and Planning Experience in Tanzania." In Michael Safier, ed., _The Role of Urban and Regional Planning in National Development of East Africa_. Kampala: Milton Obote Foundation, 1970.

Molohan, M.J.B. _Detribalization_. Dar es Salaam: Government Printer, 1959.

Nelson, Joan. _Migrants, Urban Poverty, and Instability in Developing Nations_. Center for International Affairs, Harvard University, September 1969. [Occasional Papers in International Affairs, No. 22]

Nyerere, Julius. _Decentralization_. Dar es Salaam: Government Printer, 1972.

_____. _Freedom and Socialism_. Nairobi: Oxford University Press, 1968.

_____. _Ujamaa: Essays on Socialism_. Dar es Salaam: Oxford University Press, 1968.

O'Barr, Jean F. "Cell Leaders in Tanzania," _African Studies Review_, Vol. 15, No. 3 (December 1972), pp. 437-65.

Ominde, S.H., and Ejiogu, C.N., eds. Population Growth and
    Economic Development in Africa. London: Heinemann, 1972.

Powell, Sandra. "Political Participation in the Barriadas:
    A Case Study," Comparative Political Studies, Vol. 2, No. 2
    (July 1969), pp. 195-215.

A Proposal for an Urban Development Corporation in Tanzania.
    Prepared by PADCO, Inc., 1969.

Quorro, J.S. "The Modern Local Leadership and the Problem of
    Effectiveness." Unpublished dissertation. University
    College, Dar es Salaam, March 1969.

Ray, Talton F. The Politics of the Barrios of Venezuela.
    Berkeley and Los Angeles: University of California Press,
    1969.

Rempel, Henry. "Labor Migration into Urban Centers and Urban
    Unemployment in Kenya." Unpublished dissertation. Univer-
    sity of Wisconsin, 1971.

_____, and Todaro, Michael P. "Rural-to-Urban Labour Migra-
    tion in Kenya." In S.H. Ominde and C.N. Ejiogu, eds.,
    Population Growth and Economic Development in Africa.

Ross, Marc. The Political Integration of Urban Squatters.
    Evanston: Northwestern University Press, 1973.

Rosser, Colin. Urbanization in Tropical Africa: A Demographic
    Introduction. New York: Ford Foundation International
    Urbanization Survey, 1972.

_____. "Action Planning in Calcutta: The Problem of Com-
    munity Participation," Journal of Development Studies,
    Vol. 8, No. 3 (April 1972), pp. 121-39.

Sabot, Richard H. Urban Migration in Tanzania. The National
    Urban Mobility, Employment and Income Survey of Tanzania,
    Volume II. University of Dar es Salaam: Economic Research
    Bureau, 1972.

_____. "Education, Income Distribution, and Rates of Urban
    Migration in Tanzania." University of Dar es Salaam,
    Economic Research Bureau Paper 72.6, September 1972.

Safier, Michael, ed. The Role of Urban and Regional Planning in
    National Development of East Africa. Kampala: Milton Obote
    Foundation, 1970.

Singer, Hans, and Jolly, Richard. "Unemployment in an African

Setting: Lessons of the Employment Strategy Mission to Kenya." In Employment in Africa: Some Critical Issues.

Solzbacher, Regina. "East Africa's Slum Problem: A Question of Definition." In Josef Gugler, ed., Urban Growth in Sub-saharan Africa. Kampala: Makerere University, 1969.

Southall, Aidan. "The Impact of Imperialism upon Urban Development in Africa." In Victor Turner, ed., Colonialism in Africa 1870-1960, Vol. III. Cambridge: Cambridge University Press, 1971.

Stren, Richard. "Urban Policy and Performance in Kenya and Tanzania," Journal of Modern African Studies, Vol. 13, No. 2 (June 1975).

_____. "Urban Policy in Africa: A Political Analysis," African Studies Review, Vol. 15, No. 3 (December 1972), pp. 489-516.

Sunday News (Dar es Salaam), 14 October 1962.

Sutton, J.E.G. Dar es Salaam: City, Port and Region. Dar es Salaam: Tanganyika Notes and Records, No. 71, 1970.

Temple, Frederick. "Politics, Planning and Housing Policy in Nairobi." Unpublished dissertation. Massachusetts Institute of Technology, 1973.

Therkildsen, O., and Moriarty, P. Economic Comparison of Building Materials: Survey of Dar es Salaam. Dar es Salaam: National Housing and Building Research Unit, Ministry of Lands, Housing and Urban Development, 1973.

Thorbecke, Erik. "The Employment Problem: A Critical Evaluation of Four ILO Comprehensive Country Reports," International Labour Review (1973), pp. 393-423.

Todaro, Michael P. "Income Expectations, Rural-Urban Migration and Employment in Africa." In Employment in Africa: Some Critical Issues. Geneva: International Labour Office, 1973.

Turner, John F.C. "Barriers and Channels for Housing Development in Modernizing Countries," American Institute of Planners Journal, Vol. 33 (May 1967), pp. 167-81.

_____. "Housing Priorities, Settlement Patterns, and Urban Development in Modernizing Countries," American Institute of Planners Journal, Vol. 34 (November 1968), pp. 354-63.

_____. "Uncontrolled Urban Settlement: Problems and

Policies." In Gerald Breese, ed., The City in Newly Developing Countries. Englewood Cliffs: Prentice-Hall, 1969.

Turner, Victor, ed. Colonialism in Africa 1870-1960, Vol. III. Cambridge: Cambridge University Press, 1971.

Ward, Barbara, d'Anjou, Lenore, and Runnalls, J.D., eds. The Widening Gap: Development in the 1970's. New York: Columbia University Press, 1971.

Weiner, Myron. "Urbanization and Political Protest," Civilisations, Vol. 17, Nos. 1-2 (1967), pp. 44-52.

Werlin, Herbert. "The Informal Sector: The Implications of the ILO's Study of Kenya," African Studies Review, Vol. 17, No. 1 (April 1974), pp. 205-12.

Worsley, Peter. "Frantz Fanon and the 'Lumpenproletariat.'" In Ralph Miliband and John Saville, eds., The Socialist Register 1972. London: Merlin Press, 1972.

Yahya, Saad. Tradition and Modernity in Residential Investment. University of Nairobi: Department of Land Development, 1971.

_____. "Permanence and Ephemera in Housing Development," East African Journal, Vol. 6, No. 4 (April 1969), pp. 25-29.

Official Documents

Canadian International Development Agency. Cooperation Canada, No. 16 (September/October 1974).

Great Britain. East Africa Royal Commission 1953-1955 Report. Cmd 9475. London: H.M.S.O., 1961 ed.

IDRC and INTERMET. Town Drift: Social and Policy Implications of Rural-Urban Migration in Eight Developing Countries. Ottawa, 1973.

Republic of Kenya. Sessional Paper on Employment No. 10 of 1973. Nairobi: Government Printer, 1973.

Tanzania:

   Annual Manpower Report to the President 1971. Dar es Salaam: Ministry of Economic Affairs and Development Planning, Manpower Planning Division, n.d.

   Central Statistical Bureau. Recorded Population Changes, 1948-67. Dar es Salaam, 1968.

BIBLIOGRAPHY

The Economic Survey, 1970-71. Dar es Salaam: Government
Printer, 1971.

Hali ya Uchumi wa Taifa Katika Mwaka 1972-73 [National Economic
Survey 1972-73]. Dar es Salaam: Government Printer, 1973.

Lands Division. "The Problem of Squatters in Urban Areas."
Unpublished memorandum, March 1967.

Laws of Tanzania. National Housing Corporation Act (Cap. 481).

Majadiliano ya Bunge [Hansard], 22 April-27 April 1971. Dar
es Salaam: Government Printer, 1971, col. 23.

Ministry of Lands, Housing and Urban Development. Achievement
in Ten Years of Independence. Dar es Salaam, 1971.

_____. Sites and Services Project. Dar es Salaam, 1973.

_____. Urban Housing Needs 1972-1976. Dar es Salaam:
Ardhi Planning Unit, 1971.

_____. "Report of Committee for Work Improvement," Schedule
II. Dar es Salaam, 1972.

NUMEIST (The National Urban Mobility, Employment and Income
Survey of Tanzania). See under Bienefeld.

Ripoti ya Mwaka 1967 ya Baraza la Kukaririria Kodi za Nyumba
[Annual Report, 1967 of the Rent Tribunal]. Dar es Salaam:
Government Printer, 1969.

Statistical Abstract 1966. Dar es Salaam: Government Printer,
1968.

Statistical Abstract 1970. Dar es Salaam: Government Printer,
1972.

Survey of Employment and Earnings 1970. Dar es Salaam:
Bureau of Statistics, 1972.

[Tanganyika]. African Census Report 1957. Dar es Salaam:
Government Printer, 1963.

Tanzania Second Five-Year Plan for Economic and Social Development: 1st July 1969-30th June 1974, Vol. I. Dar es Salaam:
Government Printer, 1969.

"Traditional Villages and Squatting in the City of Dar es
Salaam: The Extent of the Problem and Cost of Solution."
Memo by Commissioner for Town Planning, 1963; Dar es Salaam:
Ministry of Local Government.

BIBLIOGRAPHY

<u>Wages, Incomes, Rural Development, Investment and Price Policy</u>.
Government Paper No. 4, 1967. Dar es Salaam: Government
Printer, 1967.

United Nations. <u>Manual on Self-Help Housing</u> (1964). ST/SOA/53.

_____. <u>Social Aspects of Housing and Urban Development</u> (1967).
ST/SOA/71.

The World Bank. <u>Urbanization: Sector Working Paper</u>. Washington,
D.C., 1972.